136TH OPEN CHAMPIONSHIP
Card of the Championship Course

Hole	Par	Yards	Hole	Par	Yards
1	4	406	10	4	466
2	4	463	11	4	383
3	4	358	12	4	499
4	4	412	13	3	176
5	4	415	14	5	514
6	5	578	15	4	472
7	4	410	16	3	248
8	3	183	17	4	461
9	4	478	18	4	499
Out	36	3,703	In	35	3,718
			Total	71	7,421

THE OPEN
CHAMPIONSHIP

Aurum

Aurum Press
7 Greenland Street, London NW1 0ND

Published 2007 by Aurum Press

Copyright © 2007 R&A Championships Limited

Statistics of The 136th Open Championship produced on a
Unisys Computer System

Course map courtesy of Graham Gatches

"Shining Star Of The Open" (page 99) originally appeared
in the 24 July 2007 edition of *The Times*.

Assistance with records and research provided by Peter Lewis,
Stewart McDougall, Salvatore Johnson, and www.golfobserver.com

A CIP catalogue record for this book is available
from the British Library

ISBN-10: 1 84513 2785
ISBN-13: 978 1845 132781

Designed and produced by Davis Design
Printed in Great Britain by Purbrooks

THE OPEN CHAMPIONSHIP

WRITERS
Andy Farrell

Mike Aitken

David Davies

John Hopkins

Lewine Mair

PHOTOGRAPHERS
Getty Images

David Cannon

Stuart Franklin

Ross Kinnaird

Warren Little

Andy Lyons

Andrew Redington

Scott Halleran

Rob Harborne

Ker Robertson

Golf Editors

Steve Rose

Chief Editor

EDITOR
Bev Norwood

The Championship Committee

CHAIRMAN
Martin Kippax

DEPUTY CHAIRMAN
Rodney James

COMMITTEE

Keith Andrews	George MacGregor
David Bonsall	Jim McArthur
Gavin Caldwell	Jeremy Monroe
Charles Donald	Geoffrey Vero
Alan Holmes	Nigel Watt

ADVISORY MEMBER
Desmond Duffy
Council of National Golf Unions

CHIEF EXECUTIVE
Peter Dawson

DIRECTOR OF CHAMPIONSHIPS
David Hill

DIRECTOR OF RULES AND EQUIPMENT STANDARDS
David Rickman

The R&A is golf's world rules and development body and organiser of The Open Championship.
It operates with the consent of more than 130 national and international, amateur and professional organisations, from over 120 countries and on behalf of an estimated 30 million golfers in
Europe, Africa, Asia-Pacific and The Americas (outside the USA and Mexico). The United States
Golf Association (USGA) is the game's governing body in the United States and Mexico.

Introduction

By Martin Kippax

Chairman of the Championship Committee of The R&A

This year saw the return of The 136th Open Championship to Carnoustie. From every perspective, the Championship proved to be a great success. The weather leading up to The Open could not have been more different than 2006. The course was very green, although still reasonably hard and fast running, and was in immaculate condition, perfectly prepared by John Philp, Paul O'Connor, and their team. The players were unanimous in their praise of the course and set-up and acknowledged that in their interviews.

The eyes of the world media were on Carnoustie this year, which proved to be, arguably, the most demanding and exciting of all our Open Championship venues. Much enthusiasm and effort was shown by the Carnoustie Links Management Committee and the Carnoustie Championship Committee. Unfortunately Open week suffered from wet weather, but there was some spectacular golf played by the finest players which resulted, as in 1999, in the most dramatic of finishes.

Sunday proved to be a battle between Andres Romero, Sergio Garcia and Padraig Harrington. Rarely does golf give second chances, and when Padraig went into the Barry Burn twice on the 18th, all seemed lost for him. A wonderful up-and-down however and a near-miss by Sergio on the 18th resulted in a playoff. Eventually Padraig emerged victorious, breaking an eight-year gap in European champions since Paul Lawrie's win, again at Carnoustie, in 1999.

I must thank the Carnoustie Championship Committee and the many hundreds of volunteers for their enthusiastic assistance in running all of our qualifying events and The Open Championship itself.

Martin Kippax

Foreword

By Padraig Harrington

It has been a long road to becoming Champion Golfer of the Year. It started with an enjoyable and fulfilling amateur career, the highlights of which were representing Ireland and my three Walker Cup appearances. During this time I received great support from the Golfing Union of Ireland and The Royal and Ancient Golf Club of St Andrews.

After turning pro at 24, despite some early success, I decided that I had to change my swing and turned to the golf coach, Bob Torrance. We have both worked long and hard and I must thank Bob for his remarkable work ethic and absolute belief in me.

After working on my swing, the next step was to mentally convince myself that I could win a major. There were many people, especially in Ireland, who had that faith in me. However, my work with the sports psychologist, Bob Rotella, helped me personally gain that belief. Despite this, when that final putt dropped in the playoff, I had to mentally pinch myself that I had actually won The Open Championship. The resulting emotions were very evident in my face during the aftermath.

It was great to win at Carnoustie, which provided a test that all players appreciated. I enjoyed the challenge and the variety of shots that had to be played—from my left-handed bunker shot on the second hole of the Championship, all the way to the strategy required playing the fourth hole of the playoff.

It is going to mean a lot to Irish golf, especially to all the juniors, that they have an Open Champion of their own to look up to. We're a great country for supporting our sportspeople and I'm very proud of the backing I receive at home.

Clearly I have realised a personal dream by winning The Open Championship; however, I must look to the future. I have celebrated this victory and I hope now to build on this success and become the best player I can.

Padraig Harrington

The Venue

All Say: 'Tough But Fair'

By Andy Farrell

The Championship Course of the Carnoustie Golf Links has proven itself over its history. The 136th Open Championship, the seventh held over the Angus links, merely confirmed it.

If anywhere is to be described as "tough but fair" then it is here, and after the best players in the world had battled the beast once more in 2007, they were unanimous in the view. To some of those watching the thrilling denouement, the suggestion was that Carnoustie should host The Open every year. How different the reaction was in 1999.

Eight years before there was certainly drama, but controversy, too. With Carnoustie returning to The Open rota for the first time in 24 years, many of the leading players and Open followers alike might have been forgiven for thinking the place had been rechristened Car-Nasty. It was a triumph for the town, the Links Committee, and the greenkeeping staff to build the new roads, a smart new hotel behind the 18th green, and restore the condition of the links to prime championship state.

Except the players did not know what had hit them. Already having to contend with the elements, they found a course with fearsome rough. "Of all The Opens I've played in, this is by far the toughest set-up I've ever seen," said the then-defending champion Mark O'Meara. "Not only is the rough extremely deep and very difficult to play out of, the golf course is very narrow, too. Throw the wind on top of that, with the length of this course, it's going to be a heck of a contest to make pars."

He was right, it was a heck of a contest and par won. A score of 12 over par made the cut; O'Meara missed it, as did Masters champion Jose Maria Olazabal, Nick Faldo for the first time ever at The Open, and Sergio Garcia, the then 19-year-old who had just won his maiden title and would chase Tiger Woods at the USPGA a month later but who left Carnoustie in tears.

It may not have helped that the finish of the Championship descended into farce. Jean Van de Velde, with a three-stroke lead, fired his second

Golf has been played along the Barry Burn since the 16th century.

The fairway on the par-4 No 2 hole is a funnel through steep sand dunes.

shot right of the green, but instead of a drop from the grandstand, the ball took a freak bounce off a stanchion and landed back over the Barry Burn in horrid rough. Attempting to carry the water, Van de Velde's third splashed into the burn. He tried to play it from the water, thought better of it, dropped, hit into a bunker, and did well to make a 7. With a total of 290, six over par, he was now in a playoff with Justin Leonard and Paul Lawrie, the unheralded Scot proving victorious.

An observer who remarked that "The Open got the winner it deserved" mistook the true nature of the test and of the new champion. O'Meara had predicted: "The person who stays patient and remains calm will win." That man was Lawrie, from Aberdeen, who teed off 10 strokes from the lead but produced a brilliant 67 and then two fine birdies at the last two holes of the playoff. Lawrie had won in the wind in Qatar earlier in the year. He played superbly in the 1999 Ryder Cup and won the inaugural Dunhill Links Championship in 2001, played on a rotation of courses including Carnoustie.

He was a fine, if unexpected, champion.

Carnoustie has always been long, narrow, exposed to the elements, and a severe test of golf. Walter Hagen immediately put it in his top three courses in the world when he first played it. Michael Bonallack, before becoming secretary of The R&A, was the leading amateur at the 1968 Open and said: "When the wind is blowing, it is the toughest golf course in Britain. And when it's not blowing, it's still probably the toughest."

While golf has been played on the banks of the Barry since the 16th century, Allan Robertson first laid out a formal 10-hole course in 1842. Old Tom Morris extended it to 18 holes, and it was here that his son, Young Tom, first came to prominence by "defeating all comers" at the age of 16. James Braid revolutionised the course in 1926, with James Wright, captain of the Dalhousie Golf Club, tweaking the closing holes into the stiff finish we know today in time for the course's first Open in 1931.

It was won by Tommy Armour, a hero of World War I when he was blinded in the left eye. Although born a Scot and a graduate of Edinburgh University, he became a naturalised American but retained the stoic demeanour required of winners here and shared by Lawrie, the next Scottish-born player to win The Open in Scotland 68 years later.

In a deluge six years later, Henry Cotton won the second of his three Open titles, and the hardest of the lot, he thought, considering the course, the conditions, and that the American Ryder Cup team was present. In 1953, famously, Ben Hogan paid his only visit to The Open and took the Claret Jug back to America. His preparations were exhaustive, including walking the course backwards, from green to tee, in the evenings. He marched through the qualifying and then the Championship itself like the colossus he was. Not even the wind could deflect him. By legend, his drives at the sixth split the fairway between the bunkers and the out of bounds and found the same divot each time.

Gary Player, hitting a magnificent three-wood shot over the "Spectacles" bunkers to two feet for an eagle, still had to hold off Jack Nicklaus and Bob Charles to take the title in 1968. "It is the hardest golf course I have ever played anywhere," declared the South African. Seven years later a player whose nerve under pressure had been doubted claimed the first of five Open crowns, and eight major titles in all. Tom Watson beat Jack Newton in a playoff, birdieing the 18th for both the 72nd and the 90th hole of the Championship, but never parring the long par-3 16th.

The par-4 No 5 hole has a left-to-right dogleg, protected by bunkers.

Made famous by Ben Hogan, the par-5 No 6 hole is noted for its bunkers.

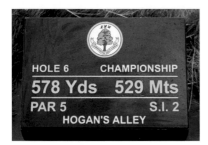

What all Carnoustie champions share are the qualities of hard work and dedication, of triumphing over adversity. Even for those who have not won, the Carnoustie experience can be rewarding. In 1999, Tiger Woods missed out on the playoff by four strokes, but the American golf writer Ron Sirak observed: "Tiger emerged as a maturer, more composed, and more complete player than ever before, one clearly excited by trying to adapt to the difficult conditions." Woods not only started an incredible sequence of major victories a month later, but returned to the 2007 Open seeking a third title in a row and a fourth in all.

Golf is in the very soul of the Angus town of Carnoustie, which lies just across the Tay Estuary from St Andrews. At the turn of the 20th century, when many emigrated from the east coast of Scotland, this wee town sent forth golfing men of note. Stewart Maiden was Bobby Jones's mentor at the East Lake course in Atlanta. Willie and Alex Smith became winners of the US Open; their brother Macdonald was one of the best players of his generation never to claim a major title.

John Philp, the long-serving head greenkeeper, is of similar stock. A Hogan devotee, he was awarded an MBE for his restoration of the links in the years before the 1999 Open. Ideal growing conditions in a spring that was warm and wet produced the jungle of rough, yet during the Championship, with a villain of the piece to be found,

Round Carnoustie

No 1 Cup • 406 yards Par 4
The opening tee shot plays into the prevailing wind, and when the wind is up, this is no easy starting hole. The drive needs to be down the left as the green is located low in a hollow, surrounded by thick rough, and with a well-bunkered ridge protecting the right-front approach.

No 2 Gulley • 463 yards Par 4
Braid's bunker in the middle of the fairway should not present a problem unless the wind is strongly against. The fairway, curving gently to the right, is a funnel through the steep sand dunes, while the green is very long and narrow, so distance control on the approach is crucial.

No 3 Jockie's Burn • 358 yards Par 4
Recently redesigned to make the tee shot more strategic on this short par-4 hole. Two bunkers jutting out from the right make this a left-to-right dogleg with either an iron to the left or a driver over the bunkers to get close to the green. But Jockie's Burn lurks on the left and in front of the green and must be considered.

No 4 Hillocks • 412 yards Par 4
Another left-to-right hole with a bunker guarding the corner of the dogleg which requires a long carry off the tee to clear. Another bunker and a ditch await left. The approach should not be long, but the green is well bunkered at the front and long enough to be shared by the 14th hole.

No 5 Brae • 415 yards Par 4
Bunkers on either side of the fairway call for an accurate tee shot, and Jockie's Burn, at 300 yards, may also come into play. The hole again doglegs left-to-right, with the long green protected by a bunker at the front and another eating into the putting surface from the left.

No 6 Hogan's Alley • 578 yards Par 5
Made famous by Ben Hogan driving down the left between the out of bounds and the bunkers in the middle of the fairway. The old bale-out area to the right of the bunkers has been tightened with the addition of two bunkers and mounding in the rough. Five bunkers around the angled green make it hard to hit from long range, so this is no easy par-5.

No 7 Plantation • 410 yards Par 4
A strong par-4 hole where out of bounds again comes into play on the left. The green has two bunkers protecting the approach and also a slight false front, so anything hit in too high has to be judged carefully.

No 8 Short • 183 yards Par 3
The course turns 90-degrees to the right for its first par-3 hole. Out of bounds remains on the left, and it is essential to hit the raised green as there is no easy up-and-down. There are two deep bunkers on the front right and two more back left.

No 9 Railway • 478 yards Par 4
This straight but narrow par-4 hole runs up towards the railway line connecting Dundee and Carnoustie. The driving area is well bunkered, with trees on the left and a ditch on the right. Club selection to the narrow green is deceptive, and this proved the hardest hole in 1999.

No 10 South America • 466 yards Par 4
Named after a Carnoustie man who set off for the said continent, but after overdoing it on his leaving party got no farther than here. The Barry Burn makes its first appearance on the back nine, cutting in front of the green and guarding the right side.

No 11 Dyke • 383 yards Par 4
A short par-4 hole running in the opposite direction to the 10th. The tee shot must be accurate to avoid bunkers both left and right, and if the rough is up, driver is not the option. The green is narrow with two bunkers on each side, so the approach needs care and precision.

No 12 Southward Ho • 499 yards Par 4
Formerly a par-5, but converted to a par-4 hole in 1999, and now playing 20 yards longer than it was eight years ago. The drive should be to the left with the approach needing to be threaded past the four bunkers at the front of a wide, shallow green which is split by a ridge.

No 13 Whins • 176 yards Par 3
A horseshoe bunker at the front of the long green makes for a visible deceptive tee shot where judgement of length is crucial. Two bunkers on the left and another on the right, while the green climbs from front to back with the tiers divided by a ridge.

No 14 Spectacles • 514 yards Par 5
A shortish par-5 by modern standards, this hole is dominated by the pair of deep bunkers 60 yards short of the blind green that give the hole its name. Two more bunkers behind the "Spectacles" guard the apron of the green, which plays as a double green with the fourth.

No 15 Lucky Slap • 472 yards Par 4
The start of a fearsome foursome to close out the Championship links. The fairway here slopes to the right, pushing ill-struck shots toward a pair of bunkers. A nest of bunkers short of the green need to be avoided on the approach. A hole not to be taken lightly.

No 16 Barry Burn • 248 yards Par 3
A mighty "short" hole, difficult when played with the prevailing wind, much worse than that if the wind is against. Hitting the plateau green, which is 46 yards long and fiendishly narrow, is the key with bunkers short left and right. A 3 here is to be cherished.

No 17 Island • 461 yards Par 4
New mounding in the rough on the right make the driving area tighter than before with the "island" fairway surrounded by the loop of the Barry Burn on three sides. The green, well-bunkered front right, has more contours than a lot of the greens, so two-putting is not a given.

No 18 Home • 499 yards Par 4
Features a new Open tee with the drive challenged by the Barry Burn, three bunkers on the right and new mounding in the rough on the left. The burn again cuts across the front of the green and was where Jean Van de Velde came to grief in 1999. As has been proved, a par here to win will be hard-earned.

Possibly the most difficult finishing hole in golf, the par-4 No 18 is defined by the Barry Burn.

Philp fitted the bill, partly due to his lack of sympathy for the leading players. "I tried to provide a challenge for the modern, stronger player with better equipment," Philp said. "They have psychologists and titanium, all I have is what God gave me. Like a lot of things in life, golf has gone soft. Golf is a character builder. It's about character and how to stand up to adversity."

Surely, Carnoustie examines these qualities like nowhere else. The test has always been to combine length with accuracy, Hogan noting that the links could not be overpowered. The bunkering is key to this. As Pat Ward-Thomas wrote: "Most of the hazards are placed to threaten the stroke that is less than perfect rather than one that is slightly better than awful." Alterations to the third and the sixth holes, as well as the tightening up of the landing areas at the final two holes, only made the requirement for precision all the greater in 2007. In addition, the course was stretched to an Open-record 7,421 yards.

But this year the rough was not nearly as thick as in 1999 despite the wet conditions during the week. Where Van de Velde had chipped from at the 18th in 1999 only whispy semi-rough lay. Alas, the Frenchman was not able to return to Carnoustie due to an illness that prevented him from qualifying. Another change was that now the links is much more familiar to players on the European Tour, thanks to the introduction of the Dunhill Links Championship, which includes Carnoustie in its rotation with Kingsbarns and the Old Course. In 2006 Ireland's Padraig Harrington won the event for the second time. In the 2007 Open programme, one of the features reviewed The Opens of 10, 20, 30, 40, and 50 years ago. Who knew they should have gone back 60 years to Irishman Fred Daly's win at Hoylake?

Carnoustie's one constant is the fiendishly winding Barry Burn that makes for such a spectacular finish at the 17th and 18th holes. Such a stage only needs to be dressed properly to allow the drama to unfold. As the players gathered for The 136th Open, any concerns they had this would not be the case were quashed by Peter Dawson, the chief executive of The R&A. "We are not seeking carnage," he declared. "We are seeking an arena where the best players can display their skills."

Exempt Competitors

Name, Country	Category
Robert Allenby, Australia	3
Stephen Ames, Canada	3, 12
Stuart Appleby, Australia	3, 13
Aaron Baddeley, Australia	3
Rich Beem, USA	11
John Bickerton, England	4
Thomas Bjorn, Denmark	4
Markus Brier, Austria	6
Paul Broadhurst, England	4
Jonathan Byrd, USA	16
Angel Cabrera, Argentina	1, 3, 4, 5, 9
Mark Calcavecchia, USA	2
Chad Campbell, USA	3, 13, 17
Michael Campbell, New Zealand	9
Paul Casey, England	3, 4, 17
K J Choi, South Korea	3
Stewart Cink, USA	3, 13, 17
Darren Clarke, Northern Ireland	17
Ben Curtis, USA	2
John Daly, USA	2
Chris DiMarco, USA	1, 3, 17
Luke Donald, England	3, 4, 13, 17
Bradley Dredge, Wales	7
Joe Durant, USA	3, 13
Pelle Edberg, Sweden	8
Johan Edfors, Sweden	4
Ernie Els, South Africa	1, 2, 3, 4
Nick Faldo, England	2
Niclas Fasth, Sweden	3, 4
Jim Furyk, USA	1, 3, 9, 13, 17, 21
Sergio Garcia, Spain	1, 3, 4, 17
Lucas Glover, USA	3
Retief Goosen, South Africa	3, 4, 9, 13
Richard Green, Australia	3
Todd Hamilton, USA	2
Anders Hansen, Denmark	3, 5
Padraig Harrington, Republic of Ireland	3, 4, 17
Gregory Havret, France	8
J J Henry, USA	17
Charles Howell III, USA	3
David Howell, England	3, 4, 5, 17
Trevor Immelman, South Africa	3, 13

Name, Country	Category
Toshi Izawa, Japan	25
Tony Jacklin, England	2
Raphael Jacquelin, France	6
Zach Johnson, USA	3, 10, 17
Robert Karlsson, Sweden	3, 4, 17
Tomohiro Kondo, Japan	25
Paul Lawrie, Scotland	2
Dong-Hwan Lee, South Korea	24
Seung-Ho Lee, South Korea	24
Tom Lehman, USA	2
Justin Leonard, USA	2
Davis Love III, USA	3, 13
Sandy Lyle, Scotland	2
Hunter Mahan, USA	15
Paul McGinley, Republic of Ireland	17
*Rory McIlroy, Northern Ireland	29
Shaun Micheel, USA	11
Phil Mickelson, USA	3, 10, 11, 12, 13, 17
Colin Montgomerie, Scotland	3, 4, 17
Toshinori Muto, Japan	24
Arron Oberholser, USA	3
Geoff Ogilvy, Australia	3, 9, 13
Nick O'Hern, Australia	3, 19
Mark O'Meara, USA	2
Rod Pampling, Australia	3, 13
Pat Perez, USA	16
Tom Pernice Jnr, USA	3
Carl Pettersson, Sweden	1, 3, 13
Ian Poulter, England	3, 4
Brett Quigley, USA	13
*Richie Ramsay, Scotland	28
Loren Roberts, USA	26
John Rollins, USA	3
Andres Romero, Argentina	1
Justin Rose, England	3
Rory Sabbatini, South Africa	3, 13
Achi Sato, Japan	24
Charl Schwartzel, South Africa	3, 4, 20
Adam Scott, Australia	1, 3, 13
Paul Sheehan, Australia	22
Jeev Milkha Singh, India	4, 18
Vijay Singh, Fiji	3, 11, 13

Name, Country	Category	Name, Country	Category
Kevin Stadler, USA	19	Anthony Wall, England	4
Henrik Stenson, Sweden	3, 4, 17	Nick Watney, USA	14
Richard Sterne, South Africa	3	*Drew Weaver, USA	27
Graeme Storm, England	7	Boo Weekley, USA	14
Steve Stricker, USA	3	Mike Weir, Canada	3, 10
Toru Taniguchi, Japan	23	Lee Westwood, England	3, 17
Hideto Tanihara, Japan	1	Brett Wetterich, USA	3, 13, 17
Vaughn Taylor, USA	3, 17	Tiger Woods, USA	1, 2, 3, 10, 11, 13, 17
David Toms, USA	3, 13, 17	Yong-Eun Yang, South Korea	6
Scott Verplank, USA	3, 17	* Denotes amateurs	

Key to Exemptions from Regional, Local Final and International Final Qualifying

Exemptions for 2007 were granted to the following:

(1) First 10 and anyone tying for 10th place in the 2006 Open Championship at Royal Liverpool.

(2) Past Open Champions aged 65 or under on 22 July 2007.

(3) The first 50 players on the Official World Golf Ranking for Week 22, 2007.

(4) First 20 in the PGA European Tour Final Order of Merit for 2006.

(5) The BMW Championship winners for 2005-2007.

(6) First 3 and anyone tying for 3rd place, not exempt having applied (3) above, in the top 20 of the PGA European Tour Order of Merit for 2007 on completion of the 2007 BMW Championship.

(7) First 2 European Tour members and any European Tour members tying for 2nd place, not exempt, in a cumulative money list taken from all official PGA European Tour events from the Official World Golf Ranking for Week 19 up to and including the Open de France and including The US Open.

(8) The leading player, not exempt having applied (7) above, in the first 10 and ties of each of the 2007 Smurfit Kappa European Open and the 2007 Barclays Scottish Open. Ties will be decided by the better final round score and, if still tied, by the better third round score and then by the better second round score. If still tied, a hole by hole card playoff will take place starting at the 18th hole of the final round.

(9) The US Open Champions for 2003-2007.

(10) The US Masters Champions for 2003-2007.

(11) The USPGA Champions for 2002-2006.

(12) The USPGA Tour Players Champions for 2005-2007.

(13) First 20 on the Official Money List of the USPGA Tour for 2006.

(14) First 3 and anyone tying for 3rd place, not exempt having applied (3) above, in the top 20 of the Official Money List of the USPGA Tour for 2007 on completion of the Crowne Plaza Invitational at Colonial.

(15) First 2 USPGA Tour members and any USPGA Tour members tying for 2nd place, not exempt, in a cumulative money list taken from the USPGA Tour Players Championship and the five USPGA Tour events leading up to and including the 2007 AT&T National.

(16) The leading player, not exempt having applied (15) above, in the first 10 and ties of each of the 2007 AT&T National and the 2007 John Deere Classic. Ties will be decided by the better final round score and, if still tied, by the better third round score and then by the better second round score. If still tied, a hole by hole card playoff will take place starting at the 18th hole of the final round.

(17) Playing members of the 2006 Ryder Cup teams.

(18) First and anyone tying for 1st place on the Order of Merit of the Asian Tour for 2006.

(19) First 2 and anyone tying for 2nd place on the Order of Merit of the Tour of Australasia for 2006.

(20) First and anyone tying for 1st place on the Order of Merit of the Southern Africa PGA Sunshine Tour for 2006/2007.

(21) The Canadian Open Champion for 2006.

(22) The Japan Open Champion for 2006.

(23) First 2 and anyone tying for 2nd place, not exempt, on the Official Money List of the Japan Golf Tour for 2006.

(24) The leading 4 players, not exempt, in the 2007 Mizuno Open. Ties will be decided by the better final round score and, if still tied, by the better third round score and then by the better second round score. If still tied, a hole by hole card playoff will take place starting at the 18th hole of the final round.

(25) First 2 and anyone tying for 2nd place, not exempt having applied (24) above, in a cumulative money list taken from all official Japan Golf Tour events from the 2007 Japan PGA Championship up to and including the 2007 Mizuno Open.

(26) The Senior British Open Champion for 2006.

(27) The Amateur Champion for 2007.

(28) The US Amateur Champion for 2006.

(29) The European Individual Amateur Champion for 2006.

(27) to (29) are only applicable if the entrant concerned is still an amateur on 19 July 2007.

Local Final Qualifying
9-10 July

Downfield
Jon Bevan, England	71	65	136
David Higgins, Rep. of Ireland	71	66	137
Scott Drummond[(P)], Scotland	72	66	138

Monifieth
David Coupland*, England	69	65	134
Paul Waring*, England	66	69	135
Llewellyn Matthews*, Wales	67	68	135

Montrose
Matthew Zions, Australia	65	68	133
David Shacklady, England	71	62	133
Justin Kehoe, Rep. of Ireland	67	68	135

Panmure
Kevin Harper, England	67	68	135
Steven Alker, New Zealand	70	65	135
Steve Parry, England	68	67	135

* Denotes amateurs   [(P)] Qualified after playoff

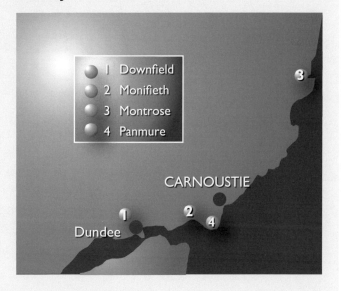

1 Downfield
2 Monifieth
3 Montrose
4 Panmure

CARNOUSTIE

Dundee

The Starting Field

"G(1) In the event of an exempt player withdrawing from the Championship or further places becoming available in the starting field after IFQ Europe and IFQ America, these places will be allocated in ranking order of entrants from the Official World Golf Ranking at the time that intimation of the withdrawal is received by the Championship Committee. Any withdrawals following the issue of OWGR Week 27 will be taken in ranking order from OWGR Week 27."

Lucas Glover, USA, replaced Shingo Katayama   Tom Pernice Jnr, USA, replaced Jose Maria Olazabal

Jon Bevan

David Coupland

David Shacklady

Kevin Harper

International Final Qualifying

ASIA
27-28 March

Sentosa			*Singapore*
Adam Groom, Australia	66	69	135
Chih Bing Lam, Singapore	70	66	136
Ross Bain, Scotland	72	64	136
David Gleeson, Australia	68	68	136
Won Joon Lee[(P)], Australia	67	70	137

Adam Groom

AMERICA
2 July

Oakland Hills			*Bloomfield Hills, Michigan*
Michael Putnam, USA	69	67	136
John Senden, Australia	66	72	138
Ryan Moore, USA	71	67	138
Charley Hoffman, USA	67	72	139
Matt Kuchar, USA	75	64	139
Anders Hultman, Sweden	70	69	139
Brian Davis, England	74	65	139
Jerry Kelly, USA	68	72	140
Sean O'Hair, USA	68	72	140
Duffy Waldorf[(P)], USA	66	75	141
Mark Hensby[(P)], Australia	66	75	141
Spencer Levin[(P)], USA	75	66	141

Michael Putnam

AUSTRALASIA
6 February

The Lakes			*Sydney, Australia*
Ewan Porter, Australia	66	69	135
Peter Fowler, Australia	74	64	138
Scott Laycock[(P)], Australia	68	73	141
Ben Bunny[(P)], Australia	71	70	141

Ewan Porter

Carnoustie

EUROPE 2 July

Sunningdale *Berkshire, England*

Graeme McDowell, N. Ireland	67	64	131
Peter Hanson, Sweden	68	65	133
Miguel Angel Jimenez, Spain	66	67	133
Nick Dougherty, England	64	69	133
Ross Fisher, England	70	64	134
Alastair Forsyth, Scotland	65	70	135
Gregory Bourdy, France	67	68	135
Oliver Wilson, England	68	67	135
Benn Barham, England	67	68	135
Fredrik Andersson Hed, Sweden	68	68	136
Mattias Eliasson, Sweden	70	66	136
Francesco Molinari, Italy	70	66	136
David Frost, South Africa	70	66	136
Mark Foster, England	66	70	136
Jose-Filipe Lima, Portugal	64	72	136
Peter Baker, England	68	68	136

Graeme McDowell

AFRICA 16-17 January

Royal Johannesburg & Kensington *Johannesburg, South Africa*

Adilson Da Silva, Brazil	66	68	134
Douglas McGuigan, Scotland	66	68	134
Desvonde Botes, South Africa	73	62	135
Terry Pilkadaris, Australia	67	68	135

Adilson Da Silva

In Celebration Of Seve

At Carnoustie in 2007, where he played his first Open Championship in 1975, Severiano Ballesteros returned to announce his retirement from competitive golf at the age of 50.

There will be no lingering swansong for Seve Ballesteros. Injuries, a ravaged swing and, ultimately, an extinguishing of desire are halting the comebacks and a seniors campaign that had hardly begun. So now there are just the memories. But such glorious memories, and so many.

"There was an internal fight," Ballesteros said. "My head say I think you should retire. My heart keep telling me to continue playing. I made probably the most difficult decision of my career as a player and I decided to retire."

Ballesteros arrived in person on the Monday at Carnoustie to "speak to you all face-to-face because I have my respect for you people" and to do it at The Open, "the best tournament in the world in my opinion." There would be courses to design and tournaments to promote, so, "definitely this is not a goodbye. This is a see you later because I will continue to be involved in the game that gave me so much over the years. I wanted to say, from my heart, thank you, and to the British people for their support.

"The people of the United Kingdom were fantastic every time. There was always a connection, a good chemistry. They really support me and I will never forget that. Most of the tournaments I won, it was because of them. I say that many times, but I wanted to say it once more.

"I have great memories," he added. "I have great memories from The Open. I hit so many good shots and so many good things happened that it's hard to describe how good I feel. It was great."

The first time Ballesteros saw a links, he wondered where on earth the course was and how you could play. But he found the British seaside was ideally suited to his style of playing the game, always aggressive, always risking trouble, but always (nearly, anyway) rescuing himself with some daring recovery and a short game bestowed by the gods.

Birkdale in 1976 was the start of his Open romance, the youngster thrilling the gallery in leading after three rounds and finishing runner-up to Johnny Miller. Then came Lytham in 1979, when even an overflow car park was no obstacle to his ability to get the ball to the hole any which way he could. US Open champion Hale Irwin's fairways-and-greens style of golf never stood a chance. Five years later he won at St Andrews, the home of golf, and against the dominant

1976 Royal Birkdale

1979 Royal Lytham

force of the time, Tom Watson. The joyful, exuberant, fist-pumping celebration became his trademark. Back at Lytham in 1988, his scintillating last round of 65 defeated the two Nicks, Faldo and Price.

Leading the tributes at Carnoustie, his old sparring partner Nick Faldo singled out that day. "I told him in the scorer's tent afterwards, 'That was the greatest round of golf I've ever seen.' We had great respect for each other," Faldo said. "Seve was golf's Cirque du Soleil. The passion, artistry, skill, drama, that was Seve.

"The last round at Lytham, the second time he won, was something special. That man was in a different state. It was the swashbuckling way he played. He hit it and chased after it and hit it, but no two follow-throughs were ever the same. You just had to stand back and admire it."

Luke Donald talked about how Faldo and Ballesteros were his twin idols growing up. Tiger Woods spoke of picking Seve's brain on several occasions about the short game. "He's probably the most creative player who has ever played the game. He was a genius," Woods said.

Ernie Els said: "There are not enough great things I can say about Seve. He was always the guy you wanted to watch, something was always going to happen."

Colin Montgomerie added: "The club just looked right in his hands. He was a natural talent. And he had a presence and that charisma. He will be missed."

Ballesteros won the Masters twice, in 1980 and 1983, and could or should have won it many more times. He won 87 titles around the world, the last of them the Spanish Open in Madrid in 1995 at the age of 38. He won the Order of Merit six times and was the driving force behind Europe's success in the Ryder Cup, both as a player and as captain in 1997 at Valderrama.

He was the Arnold Palmer of European golf, but was even more important to golf in Spain. "We have to say thank you to Seve for what he did for golf. I think the game is growing with him. As players we are proud of what he did for us," said Miguel Angel Jimenez. Sergio Garcia added: "It's sad news, but he's got to be pleased with what he's brought to the game, how he raised the level of the game, and all the things he achieved. He's had a wonderful career, one I wish I could have by the end of my days."

1984 St Andrews

For Garcia and Jimenez, the only two Spaniards in the field after Jose Maria Olazabal withdrew with a knee injury, there was now extra poignancy to their challenge at The 136th Open. And as the Championship approached, what appeared to be Ballesteros's greatest legacy was his breakthrough in winning majors and inspiring other talents such as Faldo, Bernhard Langer, Sandy Lyle, and Ian Woosnam to follow suit.

1988 Royal Lytham

Who, came the question, would "do a Seve" for the present generation of talented Europeans and end the eight-year drought going back to 1999? "Who says it won't happen this week?" said Montgomerie. "There are a few names from the Ryder Cup team that you would think would come through. It's about time a European was successful in a major championship and then it might help them all."

—**Andy Farrell**

Most Improved: It's Garcia

By Andy Farrell

There was no doubting what award the first-round leader would receive after a brilliant 65 on an eventful opening day at Carnoustie.

"Most improved, I guess," Sergio Garcia said immediately after reaching the top of the leaderboard with a 65 on the first day of The 136th Open Championship. Of course, at the major championships, they don't give out consolation awards like "most improved" or booby prizes to the poor soul who comes last. The 27-year-old Spaniard knows how it feels, however. At Carnoustie in 1999 he made a tearful departure after two days in the arms of his mother, having finished dead last. It was only a momentary blip in the fledgling career of the boy wonder, but how satisfying must it have been to return eight years later and reveal the full talents of the man he has become.

Garcia's first round at Carnoustie as a 19-year-old was an 89. He improved on that by no less than 24 strokes, but only briefly thought of that

Sergio Garcia said his 65 was 'not about revenge.'

humbling experience of memory. It came when he birdied the first hole, having hit a nine iron to eight feet. When he rolled in the putt he turned to his caddie, Glenn Murray, and said: "Well, that's four better than last time." From then on the mature professional did not allow himself any more such indulgences. "I didn't really think about it at all," he said.

"As I said at the beginning of the week," Garcia added, "this is not about revenge for me. I just want to play solid, play like I did today, give myself good looks at birdies, not suffer too much on the course, and put myself in a position to do something on Sunday. This is a good start, definitely what the doctored ordered."

With the benefit of a belly putter, which he was using for only the second tournament, Garcia made seven birdies and only dropped a shot at the long par-3 16th hole. His score was only one outside the course record. Where had the beast of a course from 1999 gone? Back then the best score anyone achieved all week was the 67 by Paul Lawrie in the final round. This time the rough was less, the condition of the course superb, and the weather

1

Not bothering with rain gear, the American Joe Durant was first off at 6.30 am and scored a par.

Greenkeeping staff were busy long before play began.

advantageous to those good enough to create their opportunities. No one was saying it was easy.

"It's the best shaped links course I've ever seen," said Garcia. "I've never seen a links where the fairways are so pure and the greens are so good." Rain helped to soften the course. It poured on Monday morning, Tuesday evening, most of Wednesday, and early on Thursday morning, an unpleasant awakening for those in the first few groups. By 9 am it was mostly a drizzle, and for the rest of the day, with only light winds, conditions were relatively benign.

"You still have to hit a lot of good shots," said Garcia. He did exactly that. He went to the turn in two-under-par 34 and did the majority of his scoring on the last nine. It was a brilliant run coming in. He holed a 30-footer at the 10th, hit a five iron to 10 feet at the 499-yard 12th, a seven iron to seven feet for a 2 at the 13th, and claimed a birdie-4 at the 14th. After the blip at the 16th, where he was bunkered, Garcia hit a six iron to 10 feet at the 17th to get back to six under par, where he finished the day two ahead of Ireland's Paul McGinley.

First Round Leaders

HOLE	1	2	3	4	5	6	7	8	9	10	11	12	13	14	15	16	17	18	
PAR	4	4	4	4	4	5	4	3	4	4	4	4	3	5	4	3	4	4	TOTAL
Sergio Garcia	③	4	4	4	4	④	4	3	4	③	4	③	②	④	4	[4]	③	4	65
Paul McGinley	③	③	4	③	4	5	③	3	4	4	4	4	②	④	[5]	[4]	4	4	67
Michael Campbell	4	③	4	③	4	④	4	3	4	[5]	4	[5]	②	④	4	[4]	③	4	68
Markus Brier	③	[5]	③	③	[6]	5	4	3	③	4	③	4	②	5	4	3	4	4	68
Angel Cabrera	4	4	4	③	4	5	③	3	4	4	4	[5]	3	④	③	3	4	4	68
*Rory McIlroy	4	4	4	4	③	5	4	3	4	③	4	4	②	5	4	3	4	4	68
Boo Weekley	③	4	[6]	4	4	④	4	②	4	4	4	4	3	④	③	3	4	4	68
K J Choi	③	4	③	③	4	④	[5]	3	4	4	4	4	②	5	[5]	3	4	[5]	69
Tiger Woods	4	4	③	4	4	③	[4]	③	4	4	[5]	[4]	5	4	②	4	4	4	69
Stewart Cink	4	4	[5]	4	4	④	4	②	③	[5]	③	4	②	5	4	[4]	4	4	69
Padraig Harrington	4	[5]	4	4	4	5	4	3	③	4	4	4	②	④	4	3	4	4	69
Miguel Angel Jimenez	4	4	4	③	4	④	4	3	4	[5]	4	4	3	④	4	3	4	4	69

* Denotes amateur

The year before, back at Hoylake, Garcia scored a 65 in the third round and went out alongside Tiger Woods in the final round. He missed a string of short putts on the opening holes and finished with a 73, seven strokes behind. This year he had missed the cut at both the Masters and the US Open. One of the best ball strikers the game possesses—witness his second place to Phil Mickelson at Sawgrass in The Players Championship—he decided his putting finally needed drastic action. He took up the belly putter of his father, Victor, a professional whose attempts to find success on the senior circuits have been plagued by the business on the greens. Vijay Singh, who also uses the implement, had made the suggestion.

"Vijay has been telling me for a year or two, but I haven't been listening," Garcia revealed. "When I feel comfortable with the short putter, I feel really good with it. But it seems to be highs and lows. I want to be more consistent. It feels like I can make a lot of putts with the belly." This longer shafted putter is anchored in the stomach and lessens the impact of the hands on the stroke.

Garcia's efforts brought the opening day to a

Garcia saved par from a bunker on No 18 to finish on six under.

Irish Amateur Scores 68

A Sparkling Debut For McIlroy

Rory McIlroy, only 18 and still an amateur, was the darling of the media after his first round of 68, which was not only three under par but the only round of the day without a bogey. What an achievement for a young man playing in his first Open and how wonderful for him that his score edged out that of his hero, Tiger Woods, by one. "It's a pretty special feeling," he said, "to say that you were better than Tiger."

Woods is now being challenged by

those whom he inspired to take up golf. When Woods won his third successive US Amateur in 1996 and days later became a professional, McIlroy was just seven years of age. "After that it was just Tiger, Tiger, Tiger," McIlroy said. "He has been the one big influence in my whole golfing life."

McIlroy has been lionised in Ireland since he started winning all their amateur events from the age of 15. He won one of the biggest, the West of Ireland championship, at 15 and 16 and began to be compared, at that tender age, to the Irish golfing greats, like the late Joe Carr.

The most remarkable shot of McIlroy's opening round was his two iron, 230 yards into the wind, to the 18th green. He missed the birdie putt but said: "If I had only one memory from the day, that would be it." That, and the standing ovation when he left the green. He had never experienced anything like it. "It was like a chill down the back of my spine," McIlroy said. "It was fantastic."

In the months before The Open, McIlroy was on the front cover of three Irish golf magazines, heady stuff for a lad not long out of school, but understandable for a nation wondering where its next Darren Clarke or Paul McGinley or Padraig Harrington was coming from.

Understandable, too, in view of some of his exploits. He won the European Individual Amateur Championship, for instance, which got him into The Open, and once, in qualifying for the North of Ireland Championship, he went round in a scarcely believable 61, 11 under par, at Royal Portrush, one of the great Irish golf courses.

The latter feat was a matter of some regret for the selection committee for the 2005 Walker Cup. It came after they had picked the team and left McIlroy out.

McIlroy remains largely unaffected by the acclaim, though, and during that wonderful first round, walking from the eighth green to the ninth tee, spotted Andrew Crone, a former schoolmate and golf partner. Crone had been carrying Tiger Woods's mobile scoreboard that day and was thus constantly in vision.

But none of that head-down, staring-at-the-ground approach for McIlroy. "Hey," he called out to his mate, "I saw you on the telly this morning," apparently oblivious to the fact that he himself was being watched by millions around the world at that very moment.

—David Davies

Players Below Par	24
Players At Par	14
Players Above Par	118

natural crescendo, helped by the startlingly performance of a young Irish amateur, Rory McIlroy, whose 68 gave him a share of third place with four others.

The morning belonged to the featured three-ball of Woods, the defending champion, Lawrie, the Carnoustie champion from 1999, and Justin Rose, who was playing in The Open for the first time since missing the cut at Royal St George's in 2003. Despite a lingering back problem, Rose had good performances at the Masters and the US Open, top-10 places in both, as well as a playoff defeat at the BMW Championship. Hopes were now again gathering towards the 26-year-old who starred as an amateur at Royal Birkdale in 1998. But he ran out of steam on the second nine and recorded a 75.

A birdie putt of about 100 feet on No 16 brought a smile to Tiger Woods's face.

Woods, on the other hand, looked imperious over the opening few holes. He birdied the third from six feet and reached the par-5 sixth with a seven iron from 207 yards, a shot of the highest class, before holing the putt from 18 feet for an eagle. At three under he was briefly tied for the lead with K J Choi, and an assault on a third consecutive title, matching Peter Thomson from 1954-56, appeared inevitable.

But the round came slightly unstuck with three bogeys around the turn, at the short eighth, the 12th, and the par-3 13th. He birdied the ninth and then holed an outrageous putt from over 80 feet at the 16th. This fearsome par-3 of 248 yards was playing into the wind, and with the hole located on the middle tier, most were only just catching the front edge. Tiger did so with a two iron and then

Excerpts FROM THE Press

"Sergio Garcia threw down the gauntlet to the rest of the field, and Tiger Woods in particular, when he took the first-round lead at The Open Championship with a spectacular round of 65, six under par at Carnoustie. … Garcia, who has been touted as a major championship winner-in-waiting since he pushed Woods all the way to the line as a 19-year-old at the USPGA Championship eight years ago, found his form at exactly the right time."

—Peter Dixon, *The Times*

"Hello world! Those famous words uttered by Tiger Woods on his professional debut in 1996 can just as easily be applied to Holywood teenager Rory McIlroy at Carnoustie. For many years Ireland has been aware of McIlroy's phenomenal talent, but he displayed it for the rest of the planet with a scintillating round of 68 on his first appearance in a major championship."

—Karl MacGinty, *Irish Independent*

"Just when you were thinking Tiger Woods was having an indifferent day, by his own high standards, he holed a putt of some 100 feet for a rare 2 at arguably the hardest par-3 in championship golf. As the roar from the huge stand behind the 16th green was heard all over the course, Woods dropped his putter, raised his arms in mock triumph, then took off his cap for a wide, sweeping bow."

—Douglas Lowe, *The Herald*

The round of 1999 champion Paul Lawrie included one of the two birdies on No 18.

whizzed his ball up the slope and into the hole before breaking out a dazzling smile. "Just made a nice shoulder turn and released it," Woods said, "and it went in the hole."

It was one of only three birdies all day at the 16th, but Lawrie went one better at the last, which yielded only two birdies. Well received in the grandstands, it got the Scot home with a 73. The only other birdie at the 18th came from Argentina's Andres Romero, who had 16 straight pars, then finished bogey-birdie for a 71. The 18th was already causing problems, but perhaps it was inevitable that a Frenchman would find it most problematic. Raphael Jacquelin twice hit approach shots out of bounds with a three wood, then switched clubs and found a greenside bunker before getting up and down for an 8, one worse than Jean Van de Velde's closing effort in 1999.

Due to the drama and the chaos of Van de Velde's finish in 1999, Lawrie does not believe he has been given the respect he deserved over the years, but this was his day in the sun, metaphorically speaking if not meteorologically. When he rolled in his putt at the last for a 3, it matched the birdie with which he finished the playoff eight years earlier. As then, he was commuting from home in Aberdeen. This time he was accompanied by his two young sons, whose days were made by the fact that they got to watch Tiger.

Clockwise from top left, Rich Beem and Luke Donald returned 70s, while K J Choi and Miguel Angel Jimenez scored 69s.

Some thought Boo Weekley's camouflage shirt was tattoos.

On 69, Padraig Harrington declared it 'a good start.'

There had been one curious incident during the round. At the 10th, Tiger's ball finished in the rough near some television cables. Usually, these are moved out of the way, unless they cannot be moved sufficiently, when they can be treated as an immoveable obstruction. The referee with the match, Alan Holmes, deemed this to be the case and offered Woods the drop. He made his par. Later, once the crowd had cleared, it was possible to move the cables, but that did not alter the fact the cables were immoveable at the time. That was hardly important on an otherwise electrifying day.

Woods was poised at two under par with a 69, sharing eighth place alongside Choi, Stewart Cink, Miguel Angel Jimenez, and Padraig Harrington. The

Stewart Cink said: 'The golf course is playing about as easy as it's going to play.'

"The last time Stewart Cink played at Carnoustie, he didn't break 80. Not Thursday, or Friday, that brazen and brutal week in 1999. The American fared considerably better during Thursday's first round of The Open as he shot two-under 69 that included five birdies."

—**Helen Ross, PGATOUR.com**

"Paul McGinley is sure to be glued to re-runs of his sizzling start to The Open—just weeks after being too de-pressed to watch golf on TV. … From a top-20 player just 18 months ago, McGinley teed up ranked 170th in the world. Not so much a fall from grace as a nosedive."

—**Iain Macfarlane, *Daily Star***

"Nerves and noise combined to dent Paul Lawrie's hopes of a flying start to his Open campaign. The Aberdonian has been under intense media and public scrutiny in the build-up to his Carnoustie return. He remains in the pack after a two-over-par first round of 73."

—**Dave Edwards,
*The Press and Journal***

"Sergio Garcia went from sobs to smiles, from his worst score as a professional to his best start ever in a major championship. Thursday at The Open was quite a turnaround for him, and Carnoustie, too."

—**Doug Ferguson,
*The Associated Press***

Irishman had warmed up for The Open not at Loch Lomond for the Barclays Scottish Open but by playing in the Irish PGA Championship at the European Club, a terrific links in County Wicklow. He won it, too, just as he did the Irish Open in May, where he became the first home player to win his national title for 25 years. "It was the ideal preparation for a big event, playing four rounds in a relaxed atmosphere on a links golf course," said Harrington. "I wish I could do it for every major." A bogey at the second was not corrected until a birdie at the ninth, but coming home in 33 was encouraging for the Dubliner.

It was a marvellous day for the Irish all round. For McGinley there was the joy of his swing clicking into place on the practice range and

Round of the Day

There were only fleeting thoughts of his first round in 1999 as Sergio Garcia set out. And, instead of the 89 of eight years ago, Garcia posted 65 to be the leader on six under par.

Garcia took a three iron off the tee on the first hole, struck a nine iron to the green, and holed from eight feet. "I got off to a great start," he said. "I hit two really solid shots on the first and a wonderful putt. I got my round going from there. I managed to hit a good amount of fairways (13 of 15 on the driving holes), a good amount of greens (13 of 18), and on the back nine I started hitting it a little closer, rolling the putts in, and managed to play those last four holes on even par, which is always very nice."

He posted only one bogey against seven birdies. He managed par-4s after missing the fairways off the second and fourth tees, and was clear through No 15 without a blemish on his card. On No 16, Garcia hit a two-iron shot into the right bunker, came out to 10 feet, and missed the putt for bogey-4.

After the first hole, Garcia's birdies came on the par-5 sixth with two putts from 35 feet, on the par-4 No 10 with a 30-foot putt after a five-iron approach, on the par-4 No 12 with a five iron to 10 feet, on the par-3 No 13 on a seven iron off the tee to seven feet, on the par-5 No 14 on two putts from 65 feet, and finally on the par-4 No 17 with a six iron to 10 feet.

"There were some birdie chances out there," Garcia said. "I managed to hit some good shots and hole some putts."

then posting a 67, the early clubhouse lead. Only Garcia later got past him. McGinley has been involved in all three of Europe's last Ryder Cup victories, but from a personal high of winning the Volvo Masters in 2005, ending the season third on the Order of Merit and in the top 20 in the world, things had got pretty low. He was down to 170th on the World Ranking. "I've not been missing every cut, but I've not had any high finishes either," explained the 40-year-old former Gaelic footballer. "I've played a lot of mediocre golf. I've missed out on the big finishes and that has really hurt me."

Reviving memories of his sharing the lead with Tom Lehman after 36 holes in 1996 with a second-round 65 at Lytham, McGinley, wearing large mittens all the way round to keep his hands warm, birdied three of the first four holes and four of the first seven. Two more

Low Scores	
Low First Nine	
Paul McGinley	32
Low Second Nine	
Sergio Garcia	31
Low Round	
Sergio Garcia	65

Paul McGinley was four under par despite bogeys on Nos 15 and 16.

The new US Open champion, Angel Cabrera, went round with a single bogey on No 12 and four birdies.

Markus Brier scored a 68 with an erratic start.

Gregory Bourdy saved par here at the second.

birdies at Nos 13 and 14 were cancelled out by bogeys at the next two. "What pleases me most is not leading The Open, but being in control of my ball," he said. Harrington had helped with some advice. "My Achilles heel is trying too hard, pushing too hard, playing too aggressively," McGinley admitted. "Unless I'm playing well, patience is not one of my great traits. You have to let a score evolve and Padraig is great at that. He is one of the best in the world at that."

After this rekindling of passion came the infectious enthusiasm of youth. McIlroy warmed up for The Open by helping Ireland win the European Team Championships for the first time in 20 years. In the process his handicap went down to plus-six. The 18-year-old from Holywood—Belfast not Los Angeles—won the European Amateur in 2006 to earn an exemption at Carnoustie. He admitted to nerves teeing up alongside Jimenez and Henrik Stenson, but soon settled to the job at hand. He

The reception for Rory McIlroy on No 18 was a moment to remember.

was the only player in the field of 156 not to drop a stroke to par during the first round. Birdies at the fifth, 10th, and 13th provided the platform for a 68. It could have been better. He missed short putts at the 14th and 15th holes.

At the last he hit a two iron into the wind and on to the green. He missed the putt, but enjoyed the reception from the gallery. "It was like a chill down the back of my spine," he said. "Everyone has been so supportive. I was nervous to begin with, but then started soaking up the atmosphere and really enjoyed it." He outscored both his illustrious playing partners and also Woods, his hero since the American won his third US Amateur title in 1996. Winning the Silver Medal and emulating Rose's amateur dramatics from 1998 were his next aims.

Also on 68 were Austria's Markus Brier, America's Boo Weekley, in his first Open, the reigning US Open champion Angel Cabrera, and the 2005 US Open champion Michael Campbell. Cabrera carrying on his heroics from Oakmont, where he defeated Woods and Jim Furyk on another fiendishly difficult course, was no surprise. Campbell's place on the leaderboard raised a few eyebrows. "You are probably all surprised, aren't you?" Campbell enquired of the media after his round. "You probably are. I'm not. It's been quite a torrid last couple of years, but the most important thing I've done is stay patient over the last couple of months."

Retief Goosen was on a roll until taking 6 on No 15.

Jim Furyk scored a 70 with four birdies.

Michael Campbell wore pink with a symbol for good fortune.

Campbell, who brought the New Zealand parliament to a halt when he won at Pinehurst and Wellington to a standstill when he returned home to show off the trophy, freely admitted he had struggled for motivation after winning a major championship. "It felt hard to get up in the morning and go and play golf," he said. "It was bizarre. I knew it was all about my desire, and now I've got it back. I had achieved my lifetime goal of winning a major. Now I've got the goal of winning two, three, four majors. It took a long time to work that out." He quoted a sports psychologist who works with climbers attempting the summit of Everest. Getting to the top is not the ultimate destination. Getting back down to base camp—alive—is.

The Kiwi was another player to credit Singh for assistance. Singh had noticed Campbell's rhythm had got too quick. "It's all about rhythm and routine now," he said. Campbell was wearing a pink shirt

Round One Hole Summary

HOLE	PAR	YARDS	EAGLES	BIRDIES	PARS	BOGEYS	D.BOGEYS	HIGHER	RANK	AVERAGE
1	4	406	0	34	105	17	0	0	14	3.89
2	4	463	0	14	101	37	4	0	8	4.20
3	4	358	0	17	75	49	13	2	6	4.41
4	4	412	0	38	110	6	2	0	16	3.82
5	4	415	0	8	78	56	13	1	2	4.49
6	5	578	4	68	58	22	2	2	17	4.72
7	4	410	0	35	101	19	1	0	13	3.91
8	3	183	0	16	116	19	4	1	11	3.09
9	4	478	0	15	100	38	2	1	8	4.20
OUT	36	3703	4	245	844	263	41	7		36.73
10	4	466	0	9	78	55	11	3	2	4.49
11	4	383	1	29	107	19	0	0	12	3.92
12	4	499	0	6	82	59	7	2	4	4.47
13	3	176	0	37	103	16	0	0	15	2.87
14	5	514	4	54	85	12	0	1	18	4.70
15	4	472	1	9	94	48	4	0	7	4.29
16	3	248	0	3	90	58	5	0	5	3.42
17	4	461	0	13	112	29	2	0	10	4.13
18	4	499	0	2	67	68	14	5	1	4.71
IN	35	3718	6	162	818	364	43	11		36.99
TOTAL	71	7421	10	407	1662	627	84	18		73.73

There were a dozen players on 70, one under par, including (from left) Rod Pampling, J J Henry, and Alastair Forsyth.

In The Lead, But Not For Long

Carnoustie, a monster in 1999, received one compliment after another in the days leading up to this year's competition. Nonetheless, none of the players was inclined to think it was going to be less than a stern test. Retief Goosen was one of the first to find this out on the first day and John Daly was another. Markus Brier was a third. All made strong challenges for the lead but fell back.

Goosen had been having a torrid time in the weeks before The Open, missing the cut in five tournaments in succession, four in Europe and one in the United States. No surprise then that he made his way round Carnoustie gingerly, rather as does a man holding a very hot plate in his hands. Yet as birdies came on the sixth and seventh and the 12th and 13th, he must have thought his luck was beginning to turn. A putt on the 14th to go to five under par slid past the hole.

With nothing more than a pitching wedge in his hand, Goosen missed the par-4 15th green, admittedly not by much, and took a 6. Then less surpris-ingly he bogeyed the short 16th as well. A 70 was by no means a bad start. It was just that it could have been better.

"Unfortunately, I hit a poor shot at 15 and made double there, then made a bogey at the next," Goosen said. "It was a disap-pointing round, but overall I'm off to a half-decent start."

Those who gathered to follow Daly when he started at 12.47 pm knew what they wanted—a glimpse of the deftness and raw power in which he specialises. What they got was an even better start than Goosen's. The 1995 Open champion birdied the fifth, sixth, and 10th, and then on the 11th he holed out from 50 yards for eagle-3 with a wedge. That took him to five under par, and he was leading the Championship, creating ripples of excitement in the grandstands as his score was posted.

Just as suddenly, Daly's round went in the other direction. His drive on the 12th with a three wood ended in a horrible lie from where he could only chip out. Then he three-putted for a double-bogey 6. After taking five strokes to reach the 14th green, he three-putted again for a triple-bogey 8. Then he posted bogeys on three of the last four holes, finishing on 74.

If Goosen and Daly began well and faded somewhat, Brier's start was electric, three birdies, a bogey, and a double bogey in five holes. His tidy golf thereafter in which he had three more birdies was no surprise to those who, the previous summer, had seen him become the first Austrian to win on the European Tour. Just to prove this was no fluke, he won the Volvo China Open in April. His 68 was a good round, but his 5 on the second and 6 on the fifth cost him a share of the lead.

"I had to scramble a bit," Brier said, "but that's what you need to make a round like this."

It probably surprised few that Daly missed the cut on the next day, and Brier and Goosen continued to respectable finishes, although this week neither would challenge again for the Claret Jug.

—**John Hopkins**

The 1995 champion is a crowd favourite.

with the Maori mania symbol, which means good fortune. He only discovered he and his playing partner Darren Clarke were in matching pinks—Clarke also decked out in the same coloured trousers—when the rain stopped and their waterproofs came off.

Usually Ian Poulter sets the fashion alarm bells ringing, but the Englishman was wearing a slightly subdued, but definitely classy, olive tartan. It is part of his new clothing collection, though why he chose to launch the winter collection in Carnoustie in the summer is anyone's guess.

Some players only briefly set foot on the leaderboard. Retief Goosen was four under until he took a double-bogey 6 at the 15th. Achi Sato's four birdies in a row from the third hole only prefaced a 71 for the 36-year-old from Tokyo playing in The Open for the first time. Then there was John Daly, who birdied the 10th and holed a pitch shot from 50 yards at the 11th—after a huge drive at the nar-row but short par-4—for an eagle-2. The day's other eagle at a par-4 came from Lee Westwood who hit a five iron from 182 yards at the

John Daly's drive at No 12 resulted in a terrible lie and he took double-bogey 6.

Excerpts FROM THE Press

"Phil Mickelson, who has just one top 10 in 14 attempts at The Open Championship, bogeyed the par-4 18th and settled for an even-par 71, tied for 25th. It easily beat the 79 with which he started the 1999 Championship here."

—Jim McCabe, *The Boston Globe*

"Drew Weaver said earlier this week that he hoped to see his name on the leaderboard in his first Open, and the British Amateur champion accomplished that goal when he birdied the first two holes—'the perfect start,' he said."

**—Leonard Shapiro,
*The Washington Post***

"The great British sporting summer arrived in Carnoustie yesterday, with bells on. Shortly after what passed for dawn, the world's greatest golfers peeled back the curtains to find the town grey overhead, wet underfoot, and with heavy rain driving off the North Sea on a brisk north-easterly. Anyone uncertain exactly what is meant by 'dreich' had their answer."

—Paul Kelso, *The Guardian*

"The day after his 50th birthday, Nick Faldo matched his worst-ever score in The Open with an eight-over-par 79 at Carnoustie. Europe's Ryder Cup captain—Open champion in 1989, 1990, and 1992—is playing his first tournament of the year, having turned his attention to a new career as a television analyst in America."

—Mark Garrod, *Press Association*

Spectators knew the meaning of 'dreich' in following the morning game of Colin Montgomerie, Toshi Ozawa, and Stewart Cink.

15th and was not required to putt, something that worried him so much earlier in the year that he attended a "putting laboratory" in Birmingham.

Back to Daly, who led at five under after 11 holes. Alas, he drove into a horrible lie on the 12th and took a double-bogey 6. At the par-5 14th, the 1995 champion drove into a bunker, thinned his second into the rough, could hardly move the ball, and ended up with a triple-bogey 8. He came home in 40 with a bogey at the last for a 74 and would miss the cut the next day.

Daly's rise and fall brought back memories of Rod Pampling, the Australian who is the only man in history to lead a major championship on the first day and miss the cut the next. This he achieved at Carnoustie in 1999. Here he opened with a 70 and when asked about eight years before said: "I guess it may cross my mind tomorrow, but I'm not worried about it yet." He did not have to worry, and nor was Garcia about to repeat that unfortunate feat.

Sergio Garcia
The Second Time Around

By Mike Aitken

In Sergio Garcia's mind, he had long banished any trace of bitterness over that numbing 89 which marked his debut at Carnoustie in 1999. For a start, his record in The Open confirmed a gift for links golf—he had finished in the top five at five of the six previous championships—and he knew his misery in Angus eight years earlier was by no means a solitary regret.

At Loch Lomond for the Barclays Scottish Open the week before The Open, Garcia was reflective about how he had coped as a teenager with rounds of 89 and 83 when many expected him to contend for the Claret Jug. After all, he had won the Irish Open that summer and shredded Loch Lomond's defences with a blistering 62 which could have been 59 with a smidgen of luck.

When the 19-year-old arrived in Angus full of the joys of youth, Carnoustie brought him tumbling down to earth. At the time, he was so upset by the scuppering of high expectations that he came off the 18th green and wept on his mother's shoulder. He was a boy, and boys are easy prey for malevolent fate.

"I was a youngster at that time, I didn't play well and I wasn't happy," Garcia recalled. "Now, I didn't play well at Oakmont in the US Open last month, again I'm not happy, but it's a different deal. When the name of Carnoustie is mentioned, why should I feel regret? If you go through life like that, then why live at all? I have a chance to go back there and, hopefully, redeem myself."

Now 27, Garcia had been playing golf on Scotland's seaside courses since he was barely out of short trousers and teed up in the Scottish Boys championship at Dunbar.

"I've enjoyed links golf ever since I was 12 or 13," Garcia said. "I remember coming to Scotland as a youngster and relishing the creativity and the challenge of manufacturing shots on a links. It always seemed to go well with my way of playing."

Having also represented his country as an amateur on numerous occasions at places such as Western Gailes and shed a few tears along the way after defeats at the hands of less gifted but more seasoned

rivals, the young Spaniard was no stranger to disappointment.

Out of the fires of dismay, Garcia's resolve became burnished with ambition. He loved The Open, partly because the subtlety of the challenge suited the nuances of his game, but mainly because he loved to be loved by the knowledgeable, ebullient galleries. In America, a month or so after the disappointment of Carnoustie in 1999, he went to Medinah in Chicago and rode to the top of the USPGA leaderboard on a wave of excitement which crashed just a little short of the mark set by Tiger Woods.

In Britain, Garcia's performances in the Ryder Cup struck a chord, and many regarded him with the same affection they had once shown to Seve Ballesteros. By a twist of fate, Seve announced his retirement in Carnoustie on the Monday before the Championship began. When Garcia holed a testing five-footer for par on the 18th green in the cool of a grey evening in Carnoustie, the celebration in the grandstands of a thrilling 65, six under par, was both admiring and heartfelt.

With the galleries on his side, and an echo of Seve's dashing majesty in his shotmaking, there was no telling what Sergio might accomplish. "I love the people at The Open," Garcia said. "They are just amazing the way they treat me, and it's carried on. I'm really thankful for the British people. They've been very enthusiastic towards me and they've always cheered me on. It's always a thrill for me to come and play in front of them."

Older, wiser, and with a belly putter in his hands, Garcia made amends for 1999 by shooting a score which was an extraordinary 24 shots lower. Since he felt the curse of Carnoustie was a figment of the imagination of others—he insisted he had always liked the links but had been another victim of the course set-up—Sergio only once thought about the events of eight years previously on the course.

In conversation with his caddie, Glenn Murray, on the first hole, Garcia recalled: "When I rolled the birdie putt in, I looked at Glenn and said, well, that's four better than last time. From then on, I didn't really think about it at all."

A wonderful driver of the ball, assured ball striker, and a magician with a wedge, Garcia was more often held back in majors by his putting. In the first round at Carnoustie he used the belly putter just 27 times, kept the ball on line, and avoided the twitchy jabs which lit a crate of dynamite under his hopes of hoisting the Claret Jug at Hoylake the previous summer.

Garcia decided to make the switch from the short stick after the US Open and liked the feel of the club at Loch Lomond. "It felt good," he said. "I felt comfortable with it. I was rolling the ball nicely. I've been just trying to get the best routine for it to see where it feels most comfortable, and it looks like I'm starting to get it."

HOLE	PAR	PLAYER
36	–6	GARCIA
18	–4	McGINLEY
20	–3	CINK
36	–3	JIMENEZ
18	–3	BRIER
36	–2	FURYK
27	–2	CHOI
36	–2	WEEKLEY
28	–2	PAMPLING
25	–2	GOOSEN

UNISYS

THE OPEN CHAMPIONSHIP

THE OPEN
ww.opengolf.com

AFTER 4

PLAYER	CUML.
WOODS	–1
LAWRIE Paul	+2
ROSE	+3
POULTER	
ERPLANK	
WEIR	

Second Round

Woods Takes A Step Back

By Andy Farrell

While Sergio Garcia maintained his two-stroke advantage for the halfway lead, Tiger Woods struggled to keep alive his chance for another victory.

Tiger Woods peered over at the 18th green, not to watch how Sergio Garcia would finish his round, but to check when the players were holing out. Woods stood on the first tee just yards away and, assured that no applause was about to erupt, addressed his opening shot of the second round. It was a weird juxtaposition. As Garcia got up and down for a par at the last and a battling level-par round of 71 for a total of 136 to keep the lead in the second round of The Open Championship, Woods saw his hopes for a third successive Open title diminished in one swing.

It was an ugly swing at that. Taking an iron—for safety, as they usually say—Woods produced a low duck hook, a horridly crooked effort that whizzed away to the left and finished in the Barry Burn.

Tiger Woods struggled to 74, including this bogey on No 5.

The burn does not just threaten golfers on the 10th, the 17th and, of course, the 18th, but crosses just in front of the first tee and lurks away on the left before eventually snaking its way out into the North Sea. Like the pond at the 18th at The K Club, which Tiger managed to find with his opening tee shot at the Ryder Cup in 2006, this hazard should not be in play for the top professionals. On the left of the first the Barry Burn is out of bounds, so there was no question that Woods would have to tee it up again in front of the hotel.

A smile crossed his face, but it was a smile of embarrassment. "It was such a poor shot because the commitment wasn't there," Woods admitted. "I'd been practising a low shot on the range, but from the first tee I could reach the bunker of the right with a low one. I was trying to throw it in the air but hit a poor shot.

"It's not like you don't make bad swings in major championships," Woods added. His next tee shot found the right semi-rough and his approach was not quite close enough to save a bogey. It meant a 6 on the card. "The whole idea is not to make anything worse than a 5 and I didn't do that,

2

Second Round Leaders

HOLE	1	2	3	4	5	6	7	8	9	10	11	12	13	14	15	16	17	18	
PAR	4	4	4	4	4	5	4	3	4	4	4	4	3	5	4	3	4	4	TOTAL
Sergio Garcia	4	4	4	[5]	4	(4)	4	3	4	4	[5]	4	3	(4)	4	3	4	4	71-136
K J Choi	(3)	4	[5]	4	4	(4)	4	[4]	4	4	(3)	4	3	(4)	(3)	3	4	[5]	69-138
Miguel Angel Jimenez	4	4	4	(3)	4	5	4	3	[5]	[5]	4	4	3	(4)	4	(2)	4	4	70-139
Mike Weir	(3)	[5]	4	[5]	4	(4)	4	3	4	(3)	4	4	3	(4)	4	(2)	4	4	68-139
Jim Furyk	(3)	[5]	(3)	4	4	(4)	(3)	3	4	[5]	(3)	[5]	3	5	4	3	4	[5]	70-140
Boo Weekley	4	[5]	4	4	4	(4)	4	3	4	(3)	4	4	3	5	[5]	[4]	4	4	72-140
Andres Romero	(3)	[5]	(3)	(3)	4	(4)	4	3	[6]	4	4	[5]	3	(3)	4	3	[5]	4	70-141
Angel Cabrera	4	4	[5]	4	[5]	5	4	3	4	4	4	4	3	5	4	[4]	4	(3)	73-141
Lee Westwood	4	4	[5]	4	4	(4)	4	(2)	[5]	4	4	4	3	(3)	4	3	4	[5]	70-141
Alastair Forsyth	4	(3)	[5]	4	4	(4)	4	[4]	4	[5]	4	4	(2)	5	4	3	4	4	71-141
Retief Goosen	4	(3)	4	[5]	[5]	(4)	(3)	3	4	(3)	4	4	[4]	5	[5]	3	(3)	[5]	71-141
J J Henry	4	[5]	4	4	4	(4)	4	[4]	4	4	4	(3)	[4]	(4)	4	3	4	4	71-141

Open souvenir: Tiger's ball

although I did get one back on the next. I just said to myself that I'd made three bogeys yesterday and still shot two under. I've still got one left, I can still shoot two under."

But that is not how it worked out. Woods looked uncomfortable with his swing all day and he found it increasingly hard to shrug off the errors. Though he birdied the second, bogeys followed at the fifth and the eighth. The par-5 14th offered another shot back, but he lost it again at the last and he signed for a 74, finishing on 143 for a share of 20th place. Somehow the difference between Woods being level par for the Championship and one over seemed significant. He was seven strokes behind Garcia. Each of Tiger's previous three Open titles, starting with the first of his St Andrews' wins in 2000, came with him holding the 36-hole lead. Now, the proud new father might not be taking the Claret Jug back to his wife Elin and daughter Sam Alexis.

Garcia knew the significance of his saved par at the 18th, even though missing the putt would have still left him in front. His nearest challenger was now the South Korean K J Choi, who was two strokes behind on 138 after two rounds of 69, four under par to Sergio's six under. "It is always much sweeter to shoot par for the day rather than one over," said the Spaniard. "It sounds much better, although a 72 today in the conditions we played wouldn't be a bad score."

It was dry, at least, in stark contrast to the torrential rains and

---

Sergio Garcia protected his lead, finishing with pars here on No 17 and No 18.

Boo Weekley Discovers Smokies

Just Like Home Cookin'

Boo Weekley didn't rightly know where Scotland was, let alone Carnoustie, when he left his home in remote northwestern Florida to go overseas for the first time and play in The Open Championship.

Naturally, though, for a guy who didn't possess a passport until last year, when he had to go to Mexico and Canada to play, he was careful to take some advice. "I was told," Weekley said, after a second round of 72 had left him in contention on 140, "not to go anywhere near anything that looks like a sausage, and I ain't eatin' no fried blood either."

So that ruled out black pudding and haggis, the Scottish staples, and left Weekley with little choice but to fill up on Arbroath Smokies, a delicacy that comes from the eponymous town five miles down the road. "Well," he said, "they ain't got no sweet tea here, and they ain't got no fried chicken."

The Royal and Ancient, anxious to showcase Scottish products, invited Iain Spink (www.arbroathsmokies.net) to set up his stall. Weekley discovered it early on and re-fuelled there most days. "I've been eatin' a lotta fish," he said. "They've got some guy smokin' some right over there, probably some of the best you'll ever eat."

That was a good thing for Mr Weekley's health, for a good smokie (unlike the 20 tins of chewing tobacco he brought with him) is a healthy food. "I've been hearing about Boo," said Spink, "and I'm sure he's doing so well because of his healthy diet."

Spink wore T-shirts with different slogans, one of which was: "If you must smoke, smoke salmon," and added: "We use natural wild fish with just a wee bit of salt—no chemical additives." His stall was a big hit with the Carnoustie customers and also with the denizens of the Media Centre and the Bollinger champagne tent, which were right next door.

Weekley, with his country boy, homespun philosophy, fascinated those members of the world's media that had not met him before. Stories such as him asking Paul Lawrie, the champion of 1999, how he got into The Open (he's exempt until he is 65) abounded, and Weekley admitted later that: "I kinda stuck my foot in my mouth there, didn't I?

"I hated what I said, especially with him saying what he said a couple of days before, that he don't get no respect for his win. Then I say something like that and it's like, wham, here's a slap in your head."

But Weekley has the perfect excuse for not knowing about Lawrie, who when he won The Open was 159th in the World Ranking. "I don't keep up with no golf," he says. "I just don't. When I get through playing I go home and do something else. I don't care nothing about the stats, I just don't care who won what."

When asked if a visit to St Andrews, the home of golf, was in his plans, Weekley replied: "I didn't know it was the home of golf. I thought the home of golf was where I was from."

—David Davies

Players Below Par	19
Players At Par	13
Players Above Par	124

flash flooding occurring in the south of England. It was warmer, too, with the sun making a brief appearance mid-afternoon, although it was cold again by the time the later finishers were done. There was more wind and the hole positions were a touch more severe than the day before, so scoring was not as good, Mike Weir's 68 the best of the day. "It was more of a grinder's day," Garcia said.

Flair might appear to be the mercurial 27-year-old's dominant trait, but Garcia can do grinding, too, as he proved here. Again his ball-striking was simply superb. He had a birdie and a bogey on each nine, but parred his way around the last four holes, that devilish stretch that wrecked many a player's score. "There were some tough holes coming in against the wind and I hit a lot of good iron shots," he said.

Andres Romero was three under par through six. **Lee Westwood, on 141, took a bogey at the last.**

Garcia had been nervous at the start, attempting to follow up his low round of the day before. Like Woods he got into trouble at the first, but unlike Tiger managed to save par, although it required a stroke of utter genius to do so. He was a good 30 yards right of the green and in some thick rough, but his controlled swipe at the ball floated it over a bunker and it ran to 18 inches from the hole. "It was a bad lie and the club got tangled in the high grass, but when I saw the ball come out I thought it could be really good," Garcia recalled. "When I saw it bounce I knew it was going to be really close. More than anything it was a really nice shot because it kept me on the right mood."

But how had he got himself in that tricky situation? He was in

Retief Goosen finished on level-par 71, but that included five birdies and five bogeys.

the middle of the fairway with his tee shot and had a nine iron in his hands. Garcia put it simply: "I shanked it. It was a good solid shank."

Now this is not a word that is generally used in polite golfing company. Merely the mention of it can cause the vapours. "I'd rather you not use that word here," someone said. Garcia laughs in the face of such superstition. "I don't mind it. I don't mind it at all," he said. "In 2003 at Sun City in the final round on the first hole, I had a nine iron and shanked it way right of the green. That time I made bogey but I managed to win the tournament. It's not a bad thing."

In the clubhouse on 136, Garcia had improved exactly one shot a hole for 36 holes on his position in 1999 at Carnoustie. Then he was a 19-year-old who had only just turned professional. An 18-year-old amateur was the centre of attention on Friday morning and Rory McIlroy safely made the cut to win the Silver Medal. After his 68 on Thursday, when he finished late and was home even later after all the media requirements, McIlroy was back out early in the morning

Finding the burn on No 9 cost Rory McIlroy a double-bogey 6.

"Lee Westwood and Alastair Forsyth lead the home challenge going into the final two days after Ireland's Paul McGinley failed to maintain the sparkling form he showed when posting a four-under-par 67 in the first round."

—William Johnson, *The Daily Telegraph*

"Tiger Woods's reaction was priceless. Here is a man with everything in perspective. He massaged his forehead with his hand and smiled ruefully. Maddening game. Naturally, after his double-bogey opening, there was a birdie at the second. But there are days when even the great one has to suffer a fall. There were so many bad shots he seemed to have come up with new ways to register his disgust."

—Derek Lawrenson, *Daily Mail*

"When the sun broke through and the temperature moderated in mid-afternoon at the Carnoustie Golf Links, there was no better place to be for a golf enthusiast. Amend that: There is no better place to be for a golf enthusiast than an Open Championship. They do golf right here."

—Lorne Rubenstein,
The Globe and Mail (Toronto)

"I like to see how the holes are playing, in order of difficulty. Too much attention is focused on the players, in my view. Such mortals are here today and gone tomorrow, whereas the devilish 18th at Carnoustie may, bewilderingly, change its par value from 5 to 4 when it has visitors, but it is essentially eternal."

—Lynne Truss, *The Times*

and this time it was more of a struggle. Suddenly there were a lot more television cameras, photographers, and spectators watching his every move.

There were two birdies, five bogeys, and a double at the ninth where the youngster found the burn on the left of the green. It was a 76 and the Northern Irishman was back on 144, sharing 31st place, two over par for the Championship. "It was a bit of a struggle, but I managed to steady the ship over the last six holes and played those in level par, which is always good," he said. "I've made the cut and

Round of the **Day**

For the first eight holes of the second round, Mike Weir was not playing like a contender, then he came through with 68, three under par, for the low round of the day to share third place on 139. He missed the fairway off the tee on the first six holes, and took bogeys on the second and fourth holes, which offset his birdies on the first and sixth. His six-foot putt for par on the fourth slipped past the hole. On the par-3 eighth, Weir hit a superb shot into the green but failed on his birdie try from eight feet.

"The front nine was pretty indifferent," Weir admitted. "I hit some good shots, but then some funny ones. Starting about No 10 I found my groove, my golf swing, and really hit the ball solid on the back nine."

The turn-around began on the ninth, when Weir holed from seven feet for his par-4 to be out in level-par 36. About then, the complexion of his round changed, and he continued by rolling in a 25-foot putt for birdie on the par-4 10th hole.

More birdies followed on Nos 14 and 16. "When it's windy like this, you have to hit the ball solidly," he said, "and I was hitting the ball solidly, very well today. I had a great warm-up, then was a little indifferent."

that's proved I can compete. The Silver Medal was the goal and that would be a great achievement."

The Silver Medal is awarded to the low amateur who makes the cut. None of the other five amateurs in the field, including Richie Ramsay, the Scot who won the US Amateur in 2006, made the cut. Drew Weaver, the American from Virginia Tech, the university where a tragic shooting incident occurred in April, won the Amateur on his first experience of links golf in June, and he scored a 72 in the afternoon but failed to qualify on 148, six over par. A television film crew following Weaver on the first day had bizarrely asked one of his playing partners, Paul Casey, to move out of the way when Weaver was putting. Casey quietly suggested that he had a job to do, too, and that was trying to win The Open.

No amateur made the cut in 1999 or in 1975, so the last time the Silver Medal was awarded at Carnoustie was in 1968 when the great Michael Bonallack, now Sir Michael, took the honours. McIlroy's

Mike Weir said: 'The last nine holes I was right down the middle on every hole.'

Early Departures For Two Scots

On more than one occasion the careers of Scotsmen Colin Montgomerie and Paul Lawrie have become interwoven. Montgomerie suggested he should play with his countryman in Lawrie's first (and only) Ryder Cup in Boston in 1999. They dovetailed so well in the fourballs and foursomes that they won two and halved one of their four fourball and foursomes matches on the first two days. Even when split up, as they had to be for the singles, they both were victorious.

In the days leading up to The Open the two of them were yoked together again. Most newspapers and many magazines carried an interview with Lawrie, the champion of the last Open at Carnoustie, and those that did not secured interviews with Montgomerie, who is a brilliant subject on the eve of events when his natural intelligence and articulacy come into their own.

On the second day, they were united once more. Their starting times were only 22 minutes apart in the afternoon, and as

the day wore on both men struggled to reach the safe haven of the last two rounds. Neither did. Both finished Friday's round five over par, both having had identical scores of 73 and 74. Both may have thought they had a chance when they handed in their cards, but late in the day the cut slipped from five over par to four over and they were out.

Rounds of 73 and 74 were nothing to call home to Aberdeen about. But Lawrie's could have been so much better. If he had played the 18th on Friday as he played it on the Sunday eight years earlier, then he would not have fallen victim to the cut. Having done the difficult part of getting to one under par for his last six holes, Lawrie took a 6 on the par-4 18th. A 3, as he had on the 72nd hole in 1999, would have seen him through with shots to spare.

Lawrie, along with Justin Rose, was playing in the group with defending champion Tiger Woods, and had to contend with the mass of spectators and the security personnel who always follow him. "It didn't cost me

any shots, but it was difficult," Lawrie said.

Someone as astute as Montgomerie must have known the cut was going to be about four or five over, and so you have to assume that when he played his last five holes in one under par he thought he had done enough. Not so. He had made too many mistakes between the sixth and 13th, eight holes on which he dropped four strokes.

"We'll just have to wait and see," Montgomerie said of the cut when he finished, with nine groups still on the course. "If it doesn't make it, I battled hard. It wasn't easy. I didn't play well today. I played well yesterday, but didn't putt well at all. And I didn't play well today. So we'll just see."

That night Montgomerie climbed into his car to begin his journey southwards. Instead of playing the last rounds of The Open for the 11th time, he would watch the events unfold on television at his home in Surrey and perhaps wonder what might have been.

—**John Hopkins**

On 72, Steve Stricker made bogeys on the last two holes.

Ernie Els posted a steady round of 70 with one bogey.

playing partners had mixed fortunes. Henrik Stenson, winner of the Dubai Desert Classic and the Accenture Match Play earlier in the year, missed the cut by just one stroke on 147, but not the tee marker he smashed on the eighth tee. The angry thrash cost him £500 courtesy of a European Tour disciplinary action. He was not the only one getting frustrated. When Ernie Els missed his putt at the ninth, he uttered what they call audible obscenities in tennis. "I didn't see too many small kids and hopefully they closed their ears," said the usually calm South African. "This time I thought I'd let it all out. It's what a major does to you. I felt better afterwards." Despite his frustrations, Els returned a 70 and was still lurking on 142, level par, tied for 13th place.

Back to the McIlroy-Stenson group and their third man, Miguel Angel Jimenez. The only other Spaniard in the field after Garcia, Jimenez had a 70 after an opening 69 to be on 139, three under

Rod Pampling scored a 72 with double-bogey 6 on the fifth.

Miguel Angel Jimenez was on 139, sharing third place, three strokes behind Sergio Garcia, his countryman.

Padraig Harrington was three over par on the last nine.

and three behind in third place. At the age of 43 he continues to strike the ball better than ever, and he hit a great shot into the last which was not rewarded with a birdie. At the 16th, however, it was a different story. With the pin down on the lower tier, Jimenez hit a two iron that ran up to two inches from the hole. He could not quite see what was happening but knew from the crowd. He threw down his club and his cap in mock horror, then raised his arms.

Weir, the Masters champion in 2003, moved alongside Jimenez on three under with his 68. With the wind picking up as the Canadian left-hander made the turn in the afternoon, so did his game. His second nine of 32 was flawless, with birdies at the 10th, the 14th, and the 16th. "Starting on 10 I found my groove," he said. "I really struck the ball well, which you have to do in the wind. The way I struck the ball it felt like a 65, but I'll take a 68."

K J Choi scored one of his five birdies here at No 15.

Choi, who was lying second to Garcia, was one of only four other players to break 70. Three birdies coming home were only spoilt by having to lay up at the last and taking a 5. But the former powerlifter known as "Tank" was the only player to be under 70 both days with his pair of 69s. Raphael Jacquelin also scored a 69 which put him at one over par, although that would have been three under but for the 8 on No 18 on Thursday. Sweden's Niclas Fasth, whose form was so good coming into the Championship with fourth place at the US Open followed by a win and a second place, also had a 69 to get back to two over. His opening round of 75 included a penalty shot for his ball moving after he had addressed it. Charlie Hoffman, the 30-year-old from San Diego who won his first title on the US Tour earlier in the year and was playing The Open for the first time, had the other 69 to join Fasth and McIlroy on two over.

Despite this tee shot on No 14, Boo Weekley posted a par-4 in his round of 72.

Paul McGinley scored a 75 to be on 142.

Just behind Weir and Jimenez were Jim Furyk and Boo Weekley on 140, two under. Furyk had his second successive 70, fortified by the night before having a pizza on the High Street and then stopping for a pint at a pub. Weekley, on his first trip to Britain, was steering clear of the food and the driving on the "wrong" side, while the British press enjoyed getting to know the colourful backwoodsman from the Florida panhandle. Lee Westwood and Alastair Forsyth, the 31-year-old Scot from Paisley, led the British challenge at one under. Westwood became the first player to notch up two eagles in the Championship by following his 2 at the 15th on Thursday with a 3 at the 14th on Friday thanks to a two iron to 15 feet.

Paul McGinley, off late in the day, lost the magic from the day before and returned a 75 to fall back to level par. He was not helped, or rather did not help himself as he admitted, at the third when he tried to putt past a sprinkler head, as per European Tour rules, and the ball bounced six inches off the ground. He took a double-bogey 6. He only later realised that he could have obtained a free drop from the referee under The Royal and Ancient rules in operation for the Championship.

Watching his recovery on No 10, Jim Furyk took one of his four bogeys here.

Excerpts
FROM THE Press

"Richie Ramsay is getting ready to beef himself up in a bid to muscle his way into golf's big time. The Aberdonian amateur knows he has to get more power to add to his prowess when he turns professional later this year."

—Neil Cameron, *Daily Record*

"On a day when the wind whipped off the North Sea and sent scores soaring at Carnoustie, Mike Weir was in control. Of his putter. Of his irons. Of his game."

—Melanie Hauser, PGATOUR.com

"It was at the first hole Friday where this Open began to take shape, setting in motion the divergent fates of Sergio Garcia and Tiger Woods entering the weekend."

—Ron Green Jnr,
The Charlotte Observer

"Lee Westwood declared The Open up for grabs after creeping into contention and leading the British challenge."

—Simon Bird, *Daily Mirror*

"It was a day for curious happenings at The 136th Open at Carnoustie, where the long lost sun made a late-day cameo and Tiger Woods hit his opening tee shot out of bounds. Adding to the unexpected, Phil Mickelson missed his second consecutive cut in a major, and Sergio Garcia began the defence of his first-round lead by nearly taking out some of the fans around the first green."

—Damon Hack, *The New York Times*

This shot cost Phil Mickelson a bogey at No 12, and he missed the cut by one.

Paul Broadhurst started with two rounds on level-par 71.

Adam Scott came back with 70 after starting on 73.

There was a more startling demise from Pelle Edberg, the 28-year-old Swede who only came to prominence with a third-place finish at the European Open and fourth place at the Barclays Scottish Open just before The Open. He was three under par for the Championship with four holes to play after a birdie at the 14th, but then finished double bogey, bogey, double bogey, bogey. The six shots dropped put him back to three over. Michael Campbell, meanwhile, dropped off the leaderboard with a 78 to make the cut right on the mark at four over. Among those to qualify with nothing to spare were Luke Donald, who pulled his driver out of bounds at the sixth after being disturbed by a playing partner's caddie putting a club back in the bag, Zach Johnson, Sandy Lyle, Mark O'Meara, Ben Curtis, Tom Lehman, and Ian Poulter.

Also in for the weekend was Jon Bevan, on four over, a teaching professional from the Wessex Golf Centre and the only PGA club pro to make the cut. The 40-year-old, who qualified at Downfield, had never made the cut before in The Open and rarely in any of the other top rank professional events he has played in, but a closing 72 would make all the sacrifices worthwhile. "I love The Open and it's all about having a go," he said.

> ### It's a
> # Fact
>
> Davis Love III has the longest current streak of consecutive major championships played with 69 successive starts, beginning with The Open in 1990. Phil Mickelson is second with 54 consecutive (beginning with the 1994 US Open), followed by Vijay Singh with 53 consecutive (1994 Open), and Tiger Woods with 43 consecutive (1997 Masters). Jack Nicklaus holds the record with 122 successive starts in major championships from the 1962 Masters through the 1998 US Open.

Round Two Hole Summary

HOLE	PAR	YARDS	EAGLES	BIRDIES	PARS	BOGEYS	D.BOGEYS	HIGHER	RANK	AVERAGE
1	4	406	0	28	114	11	3	0	16	3.93
2	4	463	0	23	92	34	6	1	12	4.17
3	4	358	0	17	97	38	4	0	9	4.19
4	4	412	0	28	109	19	0	0	15	3.94
5	4	415	0	14	80	50	12	0	5	4.39
6	5	578	1	66	63	23	2	1	17	4.76
7	4	410	0	14	119	21	2	0	13	4.07
8	3	183	0	19	99	31	5	2	11	3.18
9	4	478	0	11	107	35	3	0	8	4.19
OUT	**36**	**3703**	**1**	**220**	**880**	**262**	**37**	**4**		**36.81**
10	4	466	0	13	79	49	14	1	3	4.43
11	4	383	0	28	106	19	3	0	14	3.98
12	4	499	0	7	87	53	9	0	4	4.41
13	3	176	0	10	107	39	0	0	9	3.19
14	5	514	3	75	62	13	2	1	18	4.61
15	4	472	0	9	77	58	10	2	2	4.48
16	3	248	0	8	106	39	3	0	6	3.24
17	4	461	0	8	109	35	4	0	7	4.22
18	4	499	0	5	62	65	20	4	1	4.73
IN	**35**	**3718**	**3**	**163**	**795**	**370**	**65**	**8**		**37.29**
TOTAL	**71**	**7421**	**4**	**383**	**1675**	**632**	**102**	**12**		**74.10**

Vijay Singh had 6 twice on No 18.

It was still only Friday, but the 18th hole had already claimed some significant scalps. Phil Mickelson, The Players champion who lost a playoff to Gregory Havret for the Barclays Scottish Open the week before, needed a 4 at the last to make the cut, but drove into the Barry Burn and then three-putted for a 6. Paul Lawrie, the 1999 champion, who would have made the cut with a bogey, also took a 6 to miss out. Colin Montgomerie had a 4 and missed out by one.

Others were luckier. Sean O'Hair took four to get down from a bunker for 6, but still made it at four over. Vijay Singh put his second shot out of bounds on the left and took a double bogey for the second day running—he was in the burn twice on Thursday—but was still (amazingly) in the running at one over par. And Padraig Harrington three-putted his way to a 6 to fall back to level par, but was not too distressed after a 73. "It's a disappointing finish, but it's easy to take 6 down the last, so it's not like it is out of the blue," said the Irishman. "I'm disappointed, but there is a lot of golf left in this tournament. I don't think the 6 today is going to have any effect on the outcome of the tournament." Prophetic words indeed.

At Home On The Links

South Korean Choi was well-prepared for Open conditions

By Lewine Mair

The whistling winds were not giving a solo performance on The Open's second day. If you got close enough to K J Choi on a couple of tees, you could hear him whistling, too. It was his way. He was an enviably relaxed man who was happy in his work, and never mind what the elements threw at him.

At the same time, Choi almost certainly was drawing good memories from his recent wins in the United States in the Memorial Tournament and the AT&T National.

Choi, who had a 69 on Thursday and matched it on Friday, had been intrigued by links golf long before he first came to Scotland. Growing up in South Korea, he had watched golf on television, with pride of place going to The Open.

"I remember thinking to myself that in order to play well in an Open, I had to learn to be a good bunker player and to be good in windy conditions," he said.

As Choi was growing up, there was a burgeoning interest in stars from Asia and Japan and how they were making out in the wider world, with Lu Liang Huan, from Taiwan (Republic of China), the first to make his mark. Mr Lu, as he was called, finished second behind Lee Trevino in the 1971 Open at Royal Birkdale and will forever be remembered for how he doffed his hat over and over as he walked up the 18th fairway.

Choi, who is 36, would have been too young to have enjoyed that Birkdale scenario or in 1974, when there was more of Mr Lu, as he tied for fifth place behind Gary Player at Royal Lytham and St Annes.

The next great player on the scene was Masahiro Kuramoto, from Japan,

who notched a fourth-place finish in 1982 at Royal Troon. Then came Shigeki Maruyama, also from Japan, who tied for fifth in 2002 at Muirfield. Most recently, the Japanese Hideto Tanihara tied for fifth in 2006 at Hoylake.

Choi's first Open was in 1998 at Birkdale when he opened with a 70 but had to pack his bags following a second-round 80. The following year, though, he had an entirely more productive trip. Carnoustie, the

Caddie Andy Prodger (left) guided Choi.

course, was not the most hospitable as set up that summer, but Choi felt that himself to be thrice blessed in playing with Paul Lawrie for the first two rounds. As he opened with scores of 76 and 72 to Lawrie's 73 and 74, he found himself mesmerised by Lawrie's links skills.

"At that stage in my career," said Choi, "my shots were very weak in the wind, so when I played with Paul, I learned a lot through watching how he used the wind to work for him."

In addition, Choi has learned many a lesson from Andy Prodger, his Scottish caddie. "Andy," he explained, "always tells me that you never know what you're going to get with Scottish weather, so he advises that I prepare myself for any condition."

Prodger, in his time, had caddied for such

players as Nick Faldo and Colin Montgomerie. The reason he felt at one with Choi was because "I always know where I am with him."

Where others talk of taking aim on majors, Choi tackles the subject from a rather different angle. All the time, he puts the emphasis on how he can improve: "I always ask myself, 'What do I need to do to improve?' and 'How do I need to be prepared to win a major when I have the opportunity?'

"I think," he continued, "that you need to be ready mentally, physically, and technically, and if you are not, you are not going to be able to win."

With his first-round 69 safely in the bag, Choi and Prodger started the second day with one more birdie as they read their 15-footer to perfection. There was a dropped shot at the third, where Choi was bunkered, but when it came to the sixth, Hogan's Alley, the player got up and down from another sandy hazard to bag his second birdie of the day.

Out in 36 after a three-putt green at the eighth, Choi had an inward 33 featuring back-to-back birdies at the 14th and 15th. True, he dropped a shot at the 18th as he had done on the first day, but, as he said, that had not come as a disappointment. He did not "see" a 5 on that hole as a bogey. "I consider it a good par," he said.

At Royal Troon, in 2004, Choi had been up among the leaders after opening rounds of 68 and 69 before falling away with a 74 and a 73. Three years on, and he felt better equipped to cope with the weekend. "This year," he said, "is a bit different. Back in 2004, I still didn't have the shots that I needed. Now, I have more shots in the bag." He also had double the number of excited photographers from his homeland following in his wake.

Who But The Spaniard?

By Andy Farrell

Even Steve Stricker's course record-equalling 64 could not stop Sergio Garcia from extending his lead to three strokes after three rounds.

Once more it was hard not to take your eyes off the 18th hole of Carnoustie's Championship Course. And it was still only Saturday. Padraig Harrington, continuing his struggles on the hole, flirted with the out of bounds on the left. Sergio Garcia had a chance to extend his lead even further. Australian John Senden had the greatest escape. His approach clattered into the stand on the right and the ball ricocheted across the green and was heading out of bounds on the left. But it struck the narrowest of uprights in the fencing and bounced back into play. What would Jean Van de Velde have given for a piece of luck like that eight years ago?

Carnoustie had never seen a day like it for scoring in The Open Championship. Steve Stricker equalled the course record with his 64, and 16 others were

Sergio Garcia returned a 68 and did not drop a shot.

under 70. Nearly half the field, 33 of 70 men, were at or below level-par 71. Garcia's 68 was notable for not containing a bogey, no mean feat while leading a major championship. He moved to nine under par on 204 and was ahead by three strokes, now with just one round remaining.

Stricker led the reshuffle behind the Spaniard, with the best of the chasing pack settling on three-under-par 210, three behind Stricker and six adrift of Garcia. Could one of them reel in the long-time leader? Only Ernie Els of the leading nine names on the leaderboard already possessed a major title. The others: Chris DiMarco, K J Choi, Stewart Cink, Paul McGinley, Paul Broadhurst, and Harrington had all come close in the past. All but Choi had posted third-round scores in the 60s.

But what an opportunity, surely, lay ahead for Garcia.

Possible weather problems lent the proceedings a slightly surreal atmosphere. The forecast spoke of stormy weather, the remnants of the rains that struck the south of England on Friday, hitting Angus in mid-afternoon. But it never happened, there was no repeat of the third day at Muirfield

The runner-up in 2006, Chris DiMarco scored a 66 to join the challenge again, sharing third place.

in 2002. It was dank and showery, and cloudy and grey, and what wind there was had shifted in direction just slightly, but otherwise it was a day to tame the beast that is Carnoustie.

Vijay Singh returned a 68 but was back on 211, sharing 10th place with Miguel Angel Jimenez, Mike Weir, Jim Furyk, and Andres Romero, the young Argentine who tied for eighth last year at Hoylake.

Justin Rose, who benefited from being out early in the third round in 2002, again tried his best to move back into contention with a 67. Pelle Edberg, the Swede becoming known for his colourful headbands that he has worn since starting to ski as a child, also scored 67 and, with Rose, got back to one under par on 212, in a tie for 15th place. Also on 212 were a trio of Americans, three-time and defending champion Tiger Woods and Rich Beem, both having posted 69s, and J J Henry.

Ian Poulter was on a charge but dropped four strokes in three holes from the 15th to finish with three others on 216 with a 70. It was Paul Casey's 30th birthday, but 69 could not get him back into contention, and he was on 214 with Nick Dougherty, who also scored 69, and five others.

Third Round Leaders

HOLE	1	2	3	4	5	6	7	8	9	10	11	12	13	14	15	16	17	18	TOTAL
PAR	4	4	4	4	4	5	4	3	4	4	4	4	3	5	4	3	4	4	TOTAL
Sergio Garcia	③	4	4	4	4	5	4	②	4	4	③	4	3	5	4	3	4	4	68-204
Steve Stricker	③	③	③	4	③	5	③	3	4	4	4	4	②	④	4	3	4	4	64-207
Chris DiMarco	③	4	4	③	4	④	[5]	②	4	4	③	4	3	④	4	[4]	③	4	66-210
Paul McGinley	4	③	4	③	4	5	4	3	③	4	4	4	3	④	4	[4]	4	4	68-210
Stewart Cink	③	4	4	4	4	④	4	3	4	4	4	[5]	3	④	4	3	③	4	68-210
Padraig Harrington	③	4	4	4	③	④	4	3	4	4	4	[5]	②	5	4	3	4	4	68-210
Ernie Els	4	③	4	4	4	[8]	4	②	4	4	③	③	②	5	4	②	4	4	68-210
Paul Broadhurst	③	4	③	4	4	[7]	4	3	[5]	4	4	③	3	③	4	3	③	4	68-210
K J Choi	4	③	4	4	4	[6]	4	[4]	4	4	③	4	3	5	4	3	4	[5]	72-210
Vijay Singh	4	4	③	4	4	④	4	3	4	4	4	4	3	④	4	3	4	4	68-211
Andres Romero	4	4	4	4	4	5	③	3	[5]	4	4	4	②	5	[5]	②	4	4	70-211
Jim Furyk	4	4	4	4	4	5	4	3	[5]	③	4	4	[4]	④	③	[4]	③	[5]	71-211
Mike Weir	4	③	[5]	4	4	5	③	[4]	4	4	4	4	3	④	[5]	3	4	[5]	72-211
Miguel Angel Jimenez	4	③	4	4	4	5	4	3	4	[5]	③	4	3	[7]	③	3	[5]	4	72-211

DiMarco then came in with a 66 to post the clubhouse lead at three under. He made seven birdies and had just two bogeys. The 38-year-old American had been struggling with a shoulder injury all year, but this was the perfect time to find his form. He had gone back to his old caddie, Pat O'Brien, and with his swing feeling back on plane told Pat that now he was hitting the ball where he was aiming, they had better start aiming for the flags and no longer way off to the right.

"I felt I learned the strategy of the course the last two days," DiMarco said. "I'm hitting the ball the best I have all year." In 2006 at Hoylake, DiMarco chased home Woods while grieving for his late mother. A year on and he was just happy to be in contention again. The ground being softer than the rock-hard surfaces at Hoylake helped him. "A couple of times my ball stopped a couple of yards short of bunkers, when normally if it was hard and dry it would probably have rolled in."

Stricker started off his round in a fashion that would infuse anyone with confidence. He holed from 10 feet at the first hole, 25 feet at the second,

Zach Johnson posted a 68, following two rounds of 73.

Round of the **Day**

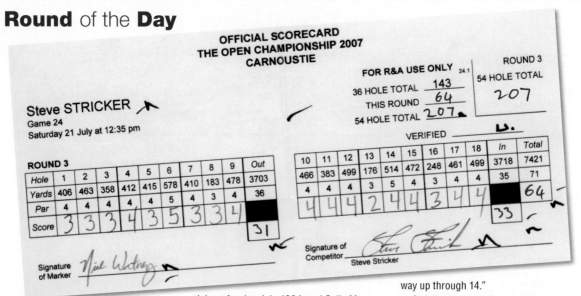

Steve Stricker planned to be more aggressive starting out in the third round. That strategy paid off with three consecutive birdies and five birdies in the first seven holes, and Stricker returned a 64, seven under par. It was the lowest score ever for an Open round at Carnoustie and also equalled the course record held by Alan Tait, a club professional, in 1994, and Colin Montgomerie, in 1995. It was tied on the last day by Richard Green.

"On the outward nine, the wind was favourable on a lot of holes," Stricker said. "I figured I needed a good round to get back into this tournament. So that was my frame of thought going out. I just tried not to get in my way as things got going well. I tried to give myself opportunities, and I did, all the way up through 14."

Stricker holed birdie putts from 10 feet at the par-4 first (after a wedge approach), 25 feet at the par-4 second (wedge), 40 feet at the third (eight iron), 20 feet at the par-4 fifth (wedge), and three feet at the par-4 seventh (seven iron), and was out in 31 strokes, five under par. "I gave myself a lot of opportunities today," he said, "and I ended up making quite a few putts."

Players Below Par	27
Players At Par	6
Players Above Par	37

and 40 feet at the third. Three birdies, three under; clearly, the work on his putting was paying off. He rolled in a 20-footer at the fifth, failed to birdie the par-5 sixth, but hit a seven iron to three feet at the seventh. He was out in 31, five under par, and his six iron to 15 feet at the short 13th set up another birdie, and he two-putted for a birdie-4 at the 14th. He had collected seven birdies, just like DiMarco, but the difference was he did not drop a shot, despite having to get up and down at each of the last four holes. Home in 33, the 64 matched the course record scores of Alan Tait and Colin Montgomerie, and in Open terms put him one ahead of Jack Newton, from the third round in 1975, and Garcia from Thursday's first round.

"I've been working on my putting and today I gave myself a lot of opportunities and they all seemed to go in," Stricker said. "I played very well from tee-to-green, especially the first 14 holes, but even after that I didn't play too badly, just couldn't quite get it on the

Steve Stricker, hitting here into No 15, had one-putt pars on the last four holes.

Three under after six holes, Padraig Harrington posted a 68, playing the next 12 holes in level par.

green. It was quite a day, quite an experience," he added. "It was a lot of fun and it gives me a chance tomorrow."

This was Stricker's first appearance in The Open since 2002. He won the Accenture Match Play in Australia in 2001, but once his wife Nicki started staying at home to bring up the children, the 40-year-old lost his desire for the game. A rededication to his career led to him recovering his card on the USPGA Tour and some fine performances in major championships. He tied for sixth and seventh in the US Open and USPGA in 2006 and tied for 13th in the 2007 US Open after contending at Oakmont.

For a Wisconsin player, missing the USPGA Tour stop in Milwaukee, which had been moved to the week of The Open, seemed strange to Stricker. "But this is a good alternative," he joked. He never thought about the course record or the major championship low of 63. "I had no idea what the records were," he said. "I was just tying to move up the leaderboard as much as I could. I was trying to get as close to Sergio as I could."

But the mood Garcia was in, that was never going to be easy. He

Paul McGinley was one of several wearing mittens to keep warm.

Excerpts
FROM THE Press

"What has encouraged me is the sturdy reaction of so many of these guys. What has encouraged them, of course, has been the relative struggles of Tiger Woods."

—**Bill Elliott,** *The Observer*

"Golf is difficult enough when you work at it, when you spend hours on the practice tee, when you drive yourself to make sure you properly drive the ball. When you don't work at it, golf is impossible. As Steve Stricker learned. As if he didn't already know."

—**Art Spander,** *Oakland Tribune*

"Rory McIlroy is guaranteed the Silver Medal as the only amateur left in the field, and yesterday he carded a solid 73 to lie four over."

—**Jock MacVicar,** *Sunday Express*

"Dazzling Dubliners Paul McGinley and Padraig Harrington were still harbouring dreams of making history today. The best pals were locked at three under, fishing to be only the second Irishman to win a major."

—**Tony Stenson,** *Daily Star Sunday*

"With the torrential rain never materialising and the wind switching to a more favourable direction, the place once dubbed 'Car-Nasty' turned into 'Car-Easy'. That was fine with Sergio Garcia, who posted a spotless 68 at Carnoustie to reach nine under par and extend his lead to three strokes."

—**Scott Michaux,** *Augusta Chronicle*

In the Words of the Competitors…

"

"The flag placements are just slightly more friendly today, and that's potentially why there's some good scores out there. The flags maybe seem to suit the wind direction somewhat."

—Justin Rose

"I'm looking forward to tomorrow. It's going to be a hard day, but hopefully one to remember."

—Sergio Garcia

"There were a couple of times today when my ball stopped within a couple of yards of bunkers. Normally if it was dry and hard, the ball probably would have rolled in them."

—Chris DiMarco

"My shots weren't that bad today. Some of the putts didn't go in. I didn't have my rhythm because it was so cold out there. I hate this kind of weather."

—K J Choi

"I hit two bad golf shots on a day that was pretty flawless, to be honest. Rather unfortunate."

—Ian Poulter

(Reason for headband) "I do a lot of skiing at home and always use it, so I thought I would use it here."

—Pelle Edberg

"

Vijay Singh returned a 68 with birdies on No 3 and the two par-5 holes, Nos 6 and 14.

Stewart Cink warned: 'There's a lot of danger lurking on Carnoustie.'

Angel Cabrera was nine strokes behind.

Andres Romero posted a 70 and was seven back.

immediately made it more difficult for the pursuers by birdieing the first hole from 11 feet. A five iron to 12 feet at the short eighth moved him to eight under. A lob wedge to 18 inches at the 11th put him at nine under. But the feature of the round was how infrequently he put himself in trouble. He was offline with his approach at the third, but got up and down with his usual panache. Otherwise he was rock steady, often switching to an iron off the tee as the wind shifted, until the 17th, where he pulled a four-iron second shot onto the bank on the left of the green.

There the ball struck a photographer on the back of the neck. This was not the first incident of the kind during the day. At the sixth hole, after birdies at the previous two holes, Woods rocketed a two iron into the crowd on the right and it hit a woman spectator on the forehead. She was treated by paramedics for a cut and for shock, and even Tiger admitted to a sickening feeling in the stomach. "She was smiling. I don't know how she could," Tiger said. "I apologised the best I could. I certainly didn't mean to hit it over there."

Back at the 17th, the man was bruised, but to Garcia's relief unblooded. "It's never a good feeling when you know you have hit someone," he said. "It's never nice. I don't recommend it to anybody. He was a little shaken, but he said numerous times he was fine, just worry about yourself." Handing over a signed glove and ball, Garcia got on with getting up and down and then at the last hit another superb long-iron shot.

"For Sergio Garcia, it is the moment of truth. Since almost the day he arrived on the golfing scene, loaded with swagger and blessed with the sweetest of swings, the young Spaniard has held the promise of a mantel full of major championship trophies."

—**Joe Logan,** *Philadelphia Inquirer*

"Steve Stricker, who lost his PGA Tour card two years ago and went begging for sponsor exemptions, has a chance to win the world's oldest golf championship. But it might take a second consecutive round like the one he played Saturday."

—**John Davis,** *The Arizona Republic*

"On a day borrowed from November, a burst of sunshine from Justin Rose. He seized the hearts and minds of those following The 136th Open Championship and wishing for a first British champion since 1999."

—**James Mossop,** *The Sunday Telegraph*

"It was a bad day for the fans as Tiger Woods and Sergio Garcia both hit spectators on the head with wayward shots."

—**Peter Higgs,** *The Mail on Sunday*

"Alastair Forsyth's third round Open jinx struck again when the Scot went from hero to zero at Carnoustie. Forsyth frittered away six shots in a re-run of his nightmare third rounds at Royal St George's in 2003 and at Royal Troon 12 months later."

—**Jim Black,** *News of the World*

The focus was directly on Garcia, who was enjoying it.

Unfortunately, he missed the putt.

Revelling in the atmosphere of The Open, Garcia had wanted to give the gallery something special there. "I wanted to make the putt on 18 for them and to hear the roar that would have been just out of this world. But it broke a little to the right," he said. It also meant the difference between a four-shot lead and being three ahead. As his second shot had soared towards the green, Garcia had shouted: "Be good, be good." He explained he usually spoke in English on the course, partly to converse with his South African caddie, Glenn Murray, and partly because he spends so much time away from Spain that "my English is becoming better than my Spanish."

While Garcia's playing partner, Choi, fell back with a 72 after losing the feeling in his hands due to the cold, plenty of others matched Garcia's 68. Among them were Harrington, Els, Cink, McGinley, and Broadhurst, who all ended up on three under alongside DiMarco. Els and Broadhurst had the most remarkable rounds playing alongside of each other. They both went out of bounds at the sixth, Els posting an 8 and Broadhurst a 7. Yet both came home in 31.

"I think everyone chasing is hoping for wind tomorrow," Els said. "Otherwise Sergio is playing so solidly, he's not making any mistakes

Twin Disasters In Hogan's Alley

What happened to Ernie Els and Paul Broadhurst at the sixth hole on the Saturday was probably not too different from what was happening to club golfers all over the country.

The two had started well enough, but when they came to Hogan's Alley, with its out-of-bounds wall on the left, Broadhurst shaped for one more solid drive—and promptly launched his ball into the adjacent field. You would have thought that Els, with his three major titles, would have been able to ignore what had happened to his playing companion, but no. He promptly followed suit, pulling his drive over the wall with room to spare.

Broadhurst went on to amass a 7, Els an 8.

Had the two of them had a couple of innocuous pars at that hole in the place of those twin disasters, Broadhurst would at that point have been no more than two shots off the lead, with Els one further back.

Luckily for them, that was where any comparisons with your Saturday amateurs stopped. Far from going from bad to worse, the two hit back. Out in 37 apiece, they each came home in 31 for a couple of 68s. At that, they were lying on 210, six behind the leader, Sergio Garcia.

Going back to that sixth hole, Broadhurst would explain: "I hadn't been hitting the ball particularly well, but I had started to feel settled. Then, I get to the sixth tee and do that. Would you believe it?" Mustering up more honesty than most, Paul admitted that it had made him feel a little better when Ernie did the same.

Els, who nowadays refuses to delve on the negative, summarised events on the sixth tee with the line: "It was just one of a couple of bad swings over the day. The rest of it was good, very good."

Els and Broadhurst are two very different golfing animals, with Els an out-and-out star and Broadhurst one who has a reputation for being a bit of a grinder, a player who puts in one solid performance after another on the European Tour without quite reaching the heights of, say, a Colin Montgomerie. Yet, on that Saturday afternoon, Broadhurst was making the same waves as Els on the homeward half. "It was great playing with Paul," said the South African. "When I started to get it going, he got it going, so we both really pulled each other along."

In spite of the gap between them and Garcia, both were still dreaming dreams of winning. When asked about Garcia and how he would handle things, Els said he wished him well, but he doubted if he would sleep easy. "I know," he said, "I've been there. It's a major, so there's still a lot that can happen."

—Lewine Mair

Paul Broadhurst struggled over the first six holes.

Ernie Els had 'a couple of bad swings.'

After two 69s, K J Choi drew a crowd while posting a 72 and saying he lost his rhythm in the cold.

Rich Beem, on 69, was tied for 15th.

and he's leading by three. It's kind of in his hands now. He is in a great position. But there's a lot of guys chasing. It's a major and there's a lot that can still happen."

McGinley chipped in on the second to restore the momentum from his opening round. "The Open for me is the greatest tournament in the world and to be in contention is a dream," said the Dubliner. "Sergio is a great front-runner. I'm well aware of how good a player he is, having been on three Ryder Cups with him. He has a big heart and I hold him in the highest esteem. It's a big task to catch him because I know what he is capable of doing."

Harrington joked that maybe he and McGinley should play their better ball against Garcia in the final round. "We might catch him that way," Harrington said. The 35-year-old Irishman birdied three of the first six holes and was then level par from there on. A worrying moment came when he flirted with the out of bounds left of the green at the 18th. It was in a similar position to where he had gone out of bounds against Stephen Dundas in the Amateur Championship in 1992, "one of the most disappointing days of my career." But all was well this time when he got up and down.

"If it had been a couple of shots better then it would have been a

Pelle Edberg was on 67, after dropping six shots late on Friday.

Justin Rose, also on 67, narrowly missed a birdie on No 18.

really good day, but I certainly take three under," Harrington said. "It's a nice return, a 68, but I feel I have a low round in me. I'm playing the right shot at the right time. If it's on, if I have the right club, the right yardage, then I'm going for the pin. If not, then I'm going for the middle of the green. There is no point being silly about it. You have to choose the right shot every time.

"It's very much in Sergio's hands," Harrington added. "It's still possible to catch him, but it depends on him. He's in control of the tournament. If he goes further under par then he's really taking everyone out. But if he makes a couple of bogeys and you make a couple of birdies, then things might change."

Finishing when and where he did, Harrington could get his media obligations done quickly and then return to his family, wife Caroline and son Patrick. "He always tells me to come back with the trophy, but he doesn't understand the pressure that's involved and that helps to take your mind off the golf and just enjoy the family time," he said.

Low Scores	
Low First Nine	
Steve Stricker	31
Low Second Nine	
Paul Broadhurst	31
Ernie Els	31
Low Round	
Steve Stricker	64

Excerpts
FROM Press
THE

"Carnoustie was the venue for Europe's most recent major success, all of eight years ago, but only after it had reduced a callow Sergio Garcia to tears. The Spaniard has a chance to put both those irritations behind him this afternoon when he takes a three-shot lead into the final round."

—Paul Forsyth, *The Sunday Times*

"At first sight you were once again alarmed by Sergio Garcia's fashion sense, but then the peseta dropped. He was wearing the orange and blood-red of Spain, and he appeared to be ready to take on all comers when he entered the bullring that was Carnoustie."

—Tim Glover,
The Independent on Sunday

"It was, bar a few putts which practically hugged the cup before abruptly withdrawing their embrace, as perfect a round as was possible under the cold but relatively benign conditions. Chris DiMarco was fluid, precise, and above all, confident in each and every stroke he unleashed."

—Mark Woods, *Scotland on Sunday*

"Masters champion Zach Johnson shot a three-under-par 68 after last week thinking he had no chance of making his mark at Carnoustie. The 30-year-old's clubs went missing during his flight from Iowa, and some hastily found replacements just didn't feel right."

—Graham Otway, *Sunday Mirror*

Tiger Woods returned a second 69, after his 74 in the second round.

Meanwhile, Garcia, as the 54-hole leader, was receiving the full grilling. The next day would be the third time he had played in the final pairing on the final day at a major championship. The previous two occasions had both ended in disappointing fashion, at the US Open at Bethpage in 2002 and The Open at Hoylake in 2006. But then both times he had been playing with Woods. Fending off questions about whether, or rather when, he is going to become a major champion has become a regular irritation for the 27-year-old. Deflecting them with his age has worked so far, but the pressure mounts. It is fair to say he knew what was coming his way. "I don't want to rekindle any bad memories…," started the first questioner, and Garcia was ready for him.

"Okay, don't. Next question please. You just said you don't want to bring bad memories. Don't ask it. Next question."

"I'm going to ask you, will you do something different this time?"

Clockwise from top left, Nick Watney, Lucas Glover, and Markus Brier all posted 70s to be on 213, level par.

3

"

"The Open for me is the greatest golf tournament in the world. To be in contention is a positive dream, being in contention going into the last round, and I've achieved that."

—Paul McGinley

"Given the opportunity tomorrow, hopefully I can keep moving up, but I'm not going to change my game plan. I was hitting the ball well today and good things happened. I need to keep doing that."

—Zach Johnson

"Conditions were probably easier than we expected. It is a tough finish there and I holed a couple of very nice putts."

—Padraig Harrington

"Nice to see it (birthday notice) on the scoreboard. It was on the messages on the right. But they didn't have to say 30th."

—Paul Casey

"Making the cut was obviously my target. When I bogeyed the last hole yesterday I didn't know if that would be one too many, but when I found out seven hours later I had made the cut, I was very pleased."

—Sandy Lyle

Mike Weir left his putt on the lip on No 13, his third miss in four holes.

"I'm not going to do anything different. I'm going to go out there and try to play my own game, just like I've been doing every single day, and believe in myself as much as possible. That's all I can do. I can only control myself. If I am in control, the way I'm hitting the ball, it's right there for the taking. Hopefully, it will be a good effort."

Later Garcia added: "The good thing about having a lead is that even if you don't have the best of starts you're still there. But if you're behind and you don't have a good start, it feels like you are falling way back. You have to attack more. I haven't been in this position

A Magical Round
Stricker Posts 64 For Carnoustie Record

The first man ever to card 64 at Carnoustie in a Championship, Steve Stricker equalled the course record set by Scots Colin Montgomerie and Alan Tait in the third round of The Open with the kind of effortlessly assured shot-making and putting which occasionally descends on a good player's game like a wizard's spell.

In recalling his own 64, Tait remembered playing the links as if in a trance. Stricker was just as taken with a performance which included seven birdies and a miserly 23 putts. "That was a magical round," acknowledged the 40-year-old from Wisconsin. "It was just one of those rounds where everything kind of went right, and my putter felt really well. I've been spending a lot of time working on my putting. I gave myself a lot of opportunities, and I ended up making quite a few putts, something that I haven't been doing of late. They all seemed to go in."

It was a display which turned the clock back for a golfer who first made his name as brilliant putter, good enough to win a World Golf Championship event, the Accenture Match Play title in 2001. A natural match-play golfer, Stricker also finished runner-up behind Vijay Singh in the USPGA Championship at Sahalee near Seattle in 1998 and twice earned spots in the top five at the US Open.

Having made his name, Stricker suddenly fell off the radar in majors

between 2003 and 2006 when he never played on the weekend. His wife Nicki, who once caddied for him, became a mother and Stricker lost his way, bedevilled by a pull hook off the tee and sense of disorientation in his private life. "When she's not there driving with you like she had been all those years, and she's taking care of the kids, and you're leaving, it tests you a little bit," he confessed. "It finds out where your heart is, and that's why I struggled."

When his game went into freefall, Stricker lost his card on the PGA Tour and admitted he didn't know what he wanted to do with his life. In the end he worked out that he was a golfer who needed to re-dedicate himself to the game, work harder, and show the desire which is part and parcel of every successful professional.

Hungry enough in 2007 to finish second to Tiger Woods at the Wachovia Championship and K J Choi at the AT&T National, as well as finish tied for 13th at Oakmont in the US Open, Stricker arrived in Angus with form and earnings for the season approaching $2.5 million. In that sense his 64 was a triumph waiting to happen, even though he

hadn't played on the links of the British Isles for five years.

It probably helped he wasn't aware of the course record and only concentrated on playing aggressively enough to claw his way back into the Championship. He made his move over Carnoustie's opening 14 holes and then defended his score over the toughest finish in championship golf. In a sense it wasn't the seven birdies which stood out in Stricker's mind, but the four pars he made between the 15th and 18th. "Anytime you can make par on those last four holes, no matter how you do it," he recalled, "it's very rewarding."

—Mike Aitken

in a major, but I'm looking forward to it. I want to play the same way I've been playing, be aggressive when I feel I can, play the right way, and hopefully it will be good enough. If somebody comes out there and shoots another 64 and beats me, hey, well done and congratulations. But I've been up there for three days and I think I've dealt with it better each day. It's tiring, but there's nothing better than seeing your name on top of the leaderboard day after day after day. It's great. I've just got to do it for one more day."

There was a light-hearted moment when he was asked if he would wear the same colours again on Sunday as he did on Saturday. The

Round Three Hole Summary

HOLE	PAR	YARDS	EAGLES	BIRDIES	PARS	BOGEYS	D.BOGEYS	HIGHER	RANK	AVERAGE
1	4	406	0	19	46	5	0	0	17	3.80
2	4	463	0	19	43	7	1	0	14	3.86
3	4	358	0	10	47	13	0	0	11	4.04
4	4	412	0	13	54	3	0	0	14	3.86
5	4	415	0	8	51	10	1	0	10	4.06
6	5	578	0	27	29	8	4	2	12	4.93
7	4	410	0	9	47	13	1	0	9	4.09
8	3	183	0	9	42	18	1	0	6	3.16
9	4	478	0	5	45	18	1	1	3	4.26
OUT	**36**	**3703**	**0**	**119**	**404**	**95**	**9**	**3**		**36.04**
10	4	466	0	5	50	14	1	0	6	4.16
11	4	383	0	13	51	6	0	0	13	3.90
12	4	499	0	5	47	15	3	0	5	4.23
13	3	176	0	16	48	6	0	0	14	2.86
14	5	514	5	40	22	1	2	0	18	4.36
15	4	472	0	4	48	15	2	1	3	4.26
16	3	248	0	4	38	28	0	0	2	3.34
17	4	461	0	10	43	17	0	0	8	4.10
18	4	499	0	3	42	21	4	0	1	4.37
IN	**35**	**3718**	**5**	**100**	**389**	**123**	**12**	**1**		**35.57**
TOTAL	**71**	**7421**	**5**	**219**	**793**	**218**	**21**	**4**		**71.61**

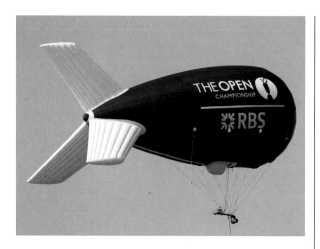

outfit was in orange and red, similar to the yellow and red of the Spanish flag, but Garcia replied: "I'll be stinky tomorrow, then." With that he went off to enjoy his mother's cooking and watch television with his family.

But it was worth recalling a moment from a press conference earlier in the week—and it was probably best he did not face the question on Saturday night—when it was put to Garcia that no one has won a major championship with the sort of longer shafted putter he was now using. "You shouldn't say that. That's no good. You guys are always trying to find something," Garcia responded. "A European hasn't won in so many years, nobody has won with a belly putter, and this and that. If I putt like I'm doing, maybe that will change soon. I don't care really. If I have to use a plastic bag to get it in the hole, I'll use whatever. So it doesn't matter."

Not Tiger's Week

By David Davies

Perhaps no one in world golf is more adept at turning a round that should, for the quality of its ball striking, add up to 80-plus into a respectable 73 or 74, than is Tiger Woods. The strength of his game in every department except off the tee is such that even with an erratic driver that often lands him deep in the rough he can rescue the situation with his superb scrambling abilities. Never has the old adage that there are four good ways of making a par-4 been more true, and Woods will almost always find a way of making par.

But even the most resilient of golfers will eventually become either so frustrated at their poor play, or at their inability to find the occasional birdie, that they find it impossible to get themselves in contention, which is what happened to Woods at Carnoustie.

He knew he had a rare opportunity to make it three Open Championships in a row, he knew he had a chance to get that little bit closer to Jack Nicklaus's record of 18 professional major championships (Woods has 12), and he knew, perhaps most pertinently, that he had the chance to take the Claret Jug home and present it to his wife Elin and to Sam Alexis, their just-born baby daughter.

That is an imposing amount of pressure even for the player of recent times who has most frequently demonstrated his ability to deal with it. But somehow it never came together. This was not a roaring Tiger. His only moment in the limelight came when he was involved in the first round in what the press call a "rules rumpus"—and even then it was not of his making.

A drive had finished, again, in the rough, and was lying close to some television cables. The usual procedure is simply to move the cables, but The R&A Rules Official, officiating for the match, declared that Woods was entitled to a free drop because the cables were immovable. He took his drop, the ball went from being out of sight to clearly in sight, although his line to the green was significantly worsened, and that, as far as Woods was concerned, was that.

But as several people including a radio reporter demonstrated, the cables could be shifted by just one pair of hands, and the occasional nonsense about special rules for Tiger began to be blathered about the place. The fact of the matter is that if the official in charge believed the cables were immovable he was perfectly entitled to give Woods a free drop, and he was completely exonerated by the rules committee.

Despite that little bit of good fortune, it soon became obvious that this was unlikely to be Tiger's week. An opening 69, two under par, was acceptable but hardly exceptional, and was notable for the fact that he hit 12 out of 15 fairways, a huge number for him.

The second round all but put him out of the Championship, and would have done but for the aforementioned scrambling ability. His opening tee shot, hit with an iron for safety, went hard left, into one of the infernal loops of the Barry Burn, where it was retrieved by a 14-year-old South African boy, Willie Smith, who turned out to be a huge Tiger fan. His disappointment at seeing his idol find the water was alleviated by his delight at going into the burn himself and snatching the ball; a unique souvenir.

The shot itself was reminiscent of the tee shot he hit off the first in the Ryder Cup at The K Club, where he also found water, and he also lost a ball in thick rough to the right of the first fairway in The Open at Royal St Georges. His Carnoustie effort was portent of what was to come. His driving was all over the place, he hit only five out of 15 fairways, three on the first nine and only two on the more difficult second nine, and no one can play that badly off the tee at Carnoustie and totally get away with it.

That Woods was able to return a score of 74 was a brilliant manifestation of his unwillingness to give in. Many of the field playing like Woods did in that round would simply have sighed, said it's not my day, and missed the cut. The Woods reaction? "That was certainly an interesting round," he said. "I didn't play all that great, I hit a lot of poor shots. I could easily have shot myself right out of the tournament today, but I hung on, I kept myself right in there."

To a point he was right. At one over par for the tournament he wasn't out of it, but he knew he required both some work on his game and two rounds over the weekend that were going to be in the mid-60s. After he had talked to the press, he said: "I'm going to the range with my coach, Hank Haney, and work on a few things. I know what I was feeling out there, and whether or not what I was feeling and what he was seeing … hopefully they'll coincide."

If they did, though, it wasn't obvious. The 69 that Woods compiled in the third round was something like three or four shots off what was needed to remind the field he was still there and in the process frighten them to death. After 54 holes Woods had only recorded nine birdies (and one eagle), a low strike rate for the world No 1.

The first question put to him when he came off the course was more of a statement. "Tiger," said his questioner, "a mixture of brilliant and frustrating play today—how would you sum it up?"

Woods replied: "You summed it up right there. Basically that was it. But if you're not at the top of your game, it's horrible, especially in a major." Woods is good at positive thinking, and he went on: "I have given myself a chance for the final round. Paul (Lawrie) came from 10 back in the final round in 1999 to win, so certainly you can do it around this golf course."

Positive thinking alone, though, cannot do it.

Pluck Of The Irish

By Andy Farrell

Padraig Harrington won a dramatic playoff against Sergio Garcia in another thrilling conclusion to an Open at Carnoustie.

Never again can any sort of lead be considered safe on these brutal links. Not for a moment. Not at Carnoustie. Sergio Garcia, the leader from day one, had it for so long, lost it, got it back so briefly, and then, cruelly, was denied at the 72nd hole as his par putt lipped out. But the young Spaniard was not the only one to suffer. Andres Romero, the sudden arrival from Argentina, felt the lash of Carnoustie's fearsome finish, and even Padraig Harrington was almost sunk at the last. Two balls in the Barry Burn and still the Irishman survived to triumph.

To the censorious who like to see their sporting champions conclude their business in a flawless fashion, and Lady Bracknell would be among them, twice finding the burn might be considered careless. But golfers know in their hearts that it is a game

---

Padraig Harrington, the first Irish champion in 60 years.

of flaws and not endless perfection. Bobby Jones, Ben Hogan, Tiger Woods, they are the exception. For the rest, from Jack Nicklaus down, it is about dealing with the errors, cleaning up the messes, not making a drama out of a crisis.

So when Harrington got up and down in two at the 72nd hole, with the name of Jean Van de Velde on his and everyone's lips, for a 6 and went on to win the four-hole playoff, that is how the 35-year-old from Dublin earned the title of "champion golfer of the year" at The 136th Open Championship. He and Garcia finished on 277, seven under par, with Harrington scoring 67, four under, and the Spaniard, 73. The margin in the playoff was 15 strokes, level par, to 16 for the four holes.

"I've proved in the past that I am capable of making things difficult for myself and still managing to win," Harrington said. Here was a man with 30 runners-up finishes to his name, including twice when he had lost playoffs to Garcia. But he also has a growing body of victories, 11 in Europe, two in America, and one in Japan in 2006 when he overhauled Woods on the final day to win in a playoff. He won the Irish Open in May in a playoff,

Fourth Round Leaders

HOLE	1	2	3	4	5	6	7	8	9	10	11	12	13	14	15	16	17	18	TOTAL
PAR	4	4	4	4	4	5	4	3	4	4	4	4	3	5	4	3	4	4	TOTAL
Padraig Harrington	4	4	(3)	4	4	(4)	4	3	(3)	4	(3)	4	3	(3)	4	3	4	[6]	67-277
	(3)															3	4	[5]	15
Sergio Garcia	4	4	(3)	4	[5]	5	[5]	[4]	4	4	4	4	(2)	(4)	[5]	3	4	[5]	73-277
	[5]															3	4	4	16
Andres Romero	4	4	(3)	(3)	4	(4)	4	(2)	[5]	(3)	(3)	[6]	(2)	(4)	(3)	(2)	[6]	[5]	67-278
Richard Green	4	(3)	(3)	4	4	(4)	4	3	(3)	4	4	4	(2)	(3)	4	3	(3)	[5]	64-279
Ernie Els	4	(3)	(3)	4	4	(4)	4	3	4	4	4	4	[4]	(4)	[5]	3	4	4	69-279
Hunter Mahan	4	4	(3)	4	4	(4)	4	3	4	(3)	(3)	4	3	(4)	4	3	(3)	4	65-280
Stewart Cink	4	4	4	(3)	4	5	4	3	[5]	4	(3)	4	3	(4)	[5]	(2)	4	[5]	70-280
Ben Curtis	4	4	(3)	4	(3)	5	4	(2)	4	(3)	4	[5]	(2)	(3)	4	3	4	4	65-281
Mike Weir	[5]	4	[5]	(3)	(3)	5	4	3	4	4	4	[5]	(2)	(4)	4	3	4	4	70-281
K J Choi	4	4	4	(3)	4	5	4	3	[6]	4	4	[5]	(2)	(4)	4	3	4	4	71-281
Steve Stricker	4	4	4	(3)	[5]	5	4	3	[5]	4	4	4	3	5	4	[4]	[5]	4	74-281

A disappointed Sergio Garcia left without the Claret Jug.

having lost a big lead and while the whole country waited desperately for their first home Open winner in 25 years. Even at the Irish PGA, against mainly club pros and aspiring tour players, the week before The Open he had a triple bogey at the 17th and needed extra time to win.

"There is nothing like having done it before," he said. "That's the greatest reason I'm here with the Claret Jug."

But it was still a shock. "I didn't know what to think," he said of watching his four-footer at the last in the playoff find the hole. "There were so many things going through my head. It was an unbelievable emotion. Am I The Open champion? What does this mean? I had a foot to watch it going in there, and it was just amazing, incredible to see it drop."

Suddenly, Harrington had become only the second Irishman to win The Open, or any major, after Fred Daly at Hoylake exactly 60 years before. "I convinced myself all week that I was going to win The Open, but I never let myself believe it," Harrington said. Few countries support their sporting figures like the Irish, and the new champion admitted: "Far

Ernie Els (left) and Paul Broadhurst (centre) were six strokes behind as they set out with their caddies.

more people had belief in me that I would become an Open champion than I ever had in myself."

What a year for Irish golf: a spectacular Ryder Cup the previous September at The K Club, Harrington becoming The Open champion, and Rory McIlroy finishing as the winner of the Silver Medal, the late Joe Carr being announced as the first Irishman to enter the World Golf Hall of Fame, and next, the Walker Cup at Royal County Down.

But Spain, in the week of Seve Ballesteros's retirement, was denied. Garcia started with a three-stroke advantage over Steve Stricker, but his long wait for a first major championship—he was so good so young—brought its own pressures. Harrington was in the pack sharing third place some six strokes behind, but Paul Lawrie had caught up 10 strokes on Van de Velde in 1999 and Tommy Armour had

been five back in 1931. At no other venue has an Open champion recovered from more than five strokes.

If the drama in 1999 had sprung up suddenly at the end, this time it built steadily throughout an enthralling day, albeit one with a wet start. Ben Curtis, the 2003 champion, and Hunter Mahan both had 65s to get to three under and four under respectively. It showed a low number was possible. Richard Green, the left-handed Australian, proved it. He started a round that would, like Stricker the day before, equal the course record with a two iron from 208 yards to four feet at the second in the worst of the driving rain. He birdied the next as well, and the sixth, and chipped in at the ninth to be out in four under.

A six iron to four feet at the 13th gave him

Excerpts FROM THE Press

Richard Green's bogey at the last cost him a share of The Open record.

another birdie and a 40-footer at the 14th an eagle. He birdied the 17th as well to get to eight under for the round and needed a par to tie The Open record of 63. But his drive just leaked into the left rough, he laid up and missed a 15-footer for his par. He was in the clubhouse on 279, five under instead of six under, but the challenge had been set. "I had my focus on shooting the course record, eight under, and that took my mind off my position in the tournament," Green said. "But I suppose I'm a bit disappointed not to be at six under and in with a better chance." He finished tied for fourth, his best result in a major.

Garcia had already extended his lead to four by birdieing the third from four feet. Stricker, inexplicably, had missed from three feet and twice more missed short putts on the outward half. His challenge evaporated in a 74. But just as Green reached the clubhouse, so Garcia's troubles began. At the fifth his tee shot finished so awkwardly on the edge of a bunker that he could only chip back to the fairway.

One shot gone but he was still in front by three, albeit appearing less calm than earlier in the week. At the next a birdie-4 eluded him

Round Four Hole Summary

HOLE	PAR	YARDS	EAGLES	BIRDIES	PARS	BOGEYS	D.BOGEYS	HIGHER	RANK	AVERAGE
1	4	406	0	4	52	11	3	0	7	4.19
2	4	463	0	11	40	15	4	0	8	4.17
3	4	358	0	18	42	9	1	0	16	3.90
4	4	412	0	11	47	11	0	1	14	4.04
5	4	415	0	11	43	12	4	0	12	4.13
6	5	578	0	13	40	12	4	1	11	5.14
7	4	410	0	6	49	12	3	0	8	4.17
8	3	183	0	9	43	15	3	0	8	3.17
9	4	478	0	6	40	18	6	0	2	4.34
OUT	**36**	**3703**	**0**	**89**	**396**	**115**	**28**	**2**		**37.26**
10	4	466	0	9	52	9	0	0	15	4.00
11	4	383	0	9	45	15	1	0	13	4.11
12	4	499	0	3	45	19	3	0	3	4.31
13	3	176	0	21	46	2	1	0	17	2.76
14	5	514	7	41	18	4	0	0	18	4.27
15	4	472	0	3	47	18	2	0	4	4.27
16	3	248	0	4	47	19	0	0	5	3.21
17	4	461	0	3	50	16	1	0	5	4.21
18	4	499	0	7	38	18	6	1	1	4.37
IN	**35**	**3718**	**7**	**100**	**388**	**120**	**14**	**1**		**35.53**
TOTAL	**71**	**7421**	**7**	**189**	**784**	**235**	**42**	**3**		**72.78**

when he missed from five feet, and now the belly putter, so secure all week, was becoming suspect. Two poor chip shots at the next two holes, two bogeys, and suddenly the whole complexion of the Championship had changed.

Now Garcia had fallen into a tie with Romero, who was putting together the round of his life. Pigu, as he is known at home, birdied the third and the fourth, hitting a wedge and a pitch stiff to the flagsticks. He holed another short putt after a three wood to the sixth, then a 15-foot putt at the eighth, but was still four strokes back at the time. A bogey at the ninth did not lose him any ground as Garcia started to struggle, and birdies at the 10th, from 25 feet, and the 11th, where he holed out from a sodden bunker, put him only two back. As he played the long par-4 12th, the deficit became one and then none.

But there was a reason the 12th took so long to play. Romero's second shot kicked right into a bush and finished unplayable. The penalty drop had to be taken over by the eighth fairway and it took an age to sort out. A double-bogey 6 was the result, and suddenly the

Hunter Mahan finished on 65.

"

"To play the first seven holes in three under par in horrible conditions was an ideal start to the day."

—Richard Green

"My first top 10. I'm very happy."

—K J Choi

"It's hard to be very pleased right now. I love this championship so much, and I did have a chance."

—Ernie Els

"I was always around the fringes this week. I never really got myself in the tournament."

—Justin Rose

"We were fortunate with the weather. By the time we got to the first tee, it was hardly raining at all."

—Jim Furyk

"The 18th hole has so much danger. It's everywhere."

—Stewart Cink

"It's been neat this week. There's been an electric atmosphere. The people truly love golf here, and they have a great time at it, and so do we as players."

—Hunter Mahan

Bogeys at No 13 and here at No 15 left Els in a fourth-place tie, two strokes behind.

26-year-old Argentine, tied for eighth on his debut in The Open in 2006, was two behind again. However, there were others for Garcia to worry about. Ernie Els, starting like a man intent on winning a first major since the 2002 Open, birdied three of the first six holes to get to six under. While further chances slipped by around the turn, his position kept improving as Garcia fell back.

The South African saved par on the 12th, but his chances faltered when his seven iron at the par-3 13th came up short in the front bunker. He took a 4, while another 4 at the 14th was not going to be enough. After a poor drive, a brilliant five iron gave him an eagle chance from 15 feet, but it did not fall. A worse drive at the next cost him a shot and he returned a 69 and joined Green in the clubhouse on 279, five under. "I got to one behind, but then lost a bit of momentum," Els said. A fifth top-four finish in The Open in six years was little consolation. "The tee shot on the 13th is the shot I'm going to look back on and not be happy about."

In the group behind Els, and two groups ahead of Garcia, Harrington made good progress early on, but remained under the radar. He pitched to four feet for a birdie at the third, got his 4 on the par-5 sixth, and holed from 15 feet for a 3 at the ninth to go out in

Andres Romero took 6 at No 12 after an unplayable lie in a bush, then scored birdies on the next four holes.

33 and lie six under, then two behind. Playing the 10th, where he saved par from 12 feet, he moved only one behind. A birdie at the 11th, from four feet, put him into a tie for the lead at seven under with Garcia and Romero.

Romero, further ahead on the course, had not disappeared after his 6 at the 12th, but merely returned to producing birdies. He said later he had a round like this back home at Mar del Plata, with nine birdies, an eagle, and "many, many bogeys." But this was The Open, and Romero's career record consisted only of one victory on Europe's Challenge Tour, two in Argentina, and one in Panama. The player ranked No 114 in the world holed from 12 feet for a 2 at the 13th, made a 4 at the 14th by getting up and down from beside the green to tie for the lead again, then went ahead with a birdie at the 15th, from 15 feet, and a 2 at the par-3 16th from 18 feet.

Now Romero stood on the 17th tee two ahead. His drive finished in the rough on the mounds on the right. The lie was not so bad

Miguel Angel Jimenez birdied the last for 71.

A disappointing 74 dropped Steve Stricker from second to joint eighth.

Mike Weir started bogey, par, bogey.

Markus Brier finished on 282.

Paul McGinley posted 283 for 19th place.

Round of the Day

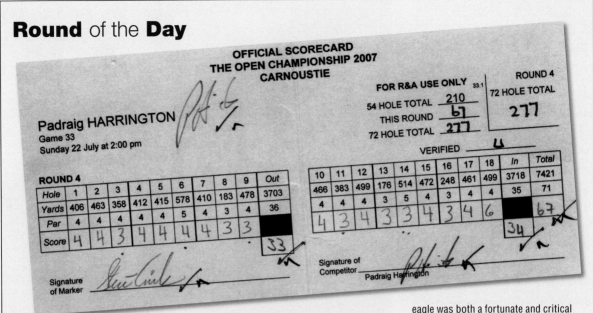

OFFICIAL SCORECARD
THE OPEN CHAMPIONSHIP 2007
CARNOUSTIE

Padraig HARRINGTON
Game 33
Sunday 22 July at 2:00 pm

FOR R&A USE ONLY 33.1
54 HOLE TOTAL ___210___
THIS ROUND ___67___
72 HOLE TOTAL ___277___

ROUND 4
72 HOLE TOTAL
277

VERIFIED ___4___

ROUND 4

Hole	1	2	3	4	5	6	7	8	9	Out
Yards	406	463	358	412	415	578	410	183	478	3703
Par	4	4	4	4	4	5	4	3	3	36
Score	4	4	3	4	4	4	4	3	3	33

Hole	10	11	12	13	14	15	16	17	18	In	Total
Yards	466	383	499	176	514	472	248	461	499	3718	7421
Par	4	4	4	3	5	4	3	4	4	35	71
Score	4	3	4	3	3	4	3	4	6	34	67

Signature of Marker

Signature of Competitor   Padraig Harrington

There were no blemishes in Padraig Harrington's four-under-par 67, except for the 6 at the par-4 final hole in regulation play, but Harrington saw no signs early on of an impending victory. "Nothing happened in the round until the 14th," he said. "I holed a good putt on 10. But besides that, nothing happened in the round that said this is my day."

Fortunately for Harrington, that "nothing" included birdies on the par-4 third, from four feet, the par-5 sixth, and the par-4 ninth, where he made a 15-footer, for him to be out in 33 strokes, three under par. He holed a par-saving putt of 12 feet on the par-4 No 10, scored his fourth birdie of the day on the par-4 No 11, then made two more pars.

Next was No 14, statistically the easiest hole of the week, the par-5 of 514 yards known as Spectacles, for the twin bunkers that mark the fairway on the left, shutting off a view of the green 70 yards away.

Harrington's approach shot to set up an eagle was both a fortunate and critical stroke in his victory. It was one of 19 eagles on that hole for the week, including seven on the last day.

"Normally, when it's your day, you chip in, you hole a long putt. None of that was happening until I got a very good break on 14," Harrington said. "I assumed my ball kicked just left of the green up there. I thought I was going to be about 30 feet away from the hole. Instead I was 15 feet away with a great chance. That was a big break, to hole that."

that he needed to chip out, but he was undecided about what club to use. His first instinct was to hit a three wood, but he changed to a two iron. The ball came out low and hooking. What happened next was unlucky by any standards. The ball hit the retaining wall of the Barry Burn as it crossed the 17th fairway and rebounded at such an angle that it shot off right and over the out-of-bounds fence on the other side of the 18th hole.

Even those who had seen it, including Romero, could not quite believe. Hitting a three wood for the replayed shot, he did brilliantly to find the green and limit the damage to a double-bogey 6. But now he was two behind and, after missing the green at the last and taking a bogey when his par-save lipped out, he was the new leader in the clubhouse on 278, six under. Three shots gone in the last two holes. His round of 67 had contained 10 birdies, two bogeys, and

Players Below Par	18
Players At Par	7
Players Above Par	45

4

Excerpts
FROM THE **Press**

"With an opportunity to do something that hadn't been done in more than half a century—win the same major championship three times in succession—Tiger Woods came up far short."

—**Vartan Kupelian,** *The Detroit News*

"There is a nine-hole golf course in Argentina's Mendoza province where the finishing hole is an exact recreation of Carnoustie's 17th. It is probably safe to assume that Andres Romero did not bother to familiarise himself with that copy before pitting himself against the real thing."

—**Alasdair Reid,** *The Daily Telegraph*

"He knew he had come up short. Six inches, to be precise. Ernie Els had taken up the chase of Sergio Garcia with an enthusiasm that belies the nickname the Big Easy. He came within one shot of the lead."

—**Hugh MacDonald,** *The Herald*

"'Although the biggest bet was only €2,000, the length and breadth of the land supported Pad in fivers, tenners, and hundreds,' reported Irish bookmaker Paddy Power. 'But we're happy to have an Irish winner.'"

—**Jeremy Chapman,** *Racing Post*

"Andres Romero came to The Open with a reputation for long hitting, inconsistency, and impetuousness under pressure and he truly lived up—and down—to all three."

—**John Huggan,** *The Guardian*

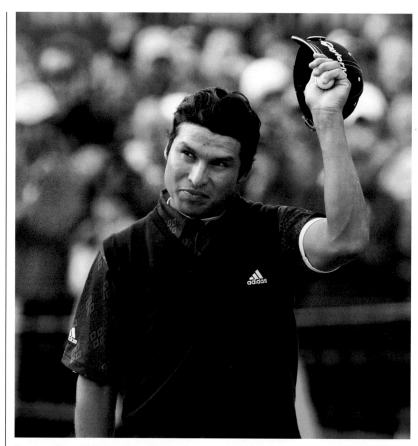

Romero tipped his hat after finishing 6-5 to fall to third place, one stroke behind.

Stewart Cink posted 70 for 280.

Ben Curtis scored a 65 for 281.

Andres Romero
One Tantalising Shot Away

When Padraig Harrington took a moment to examine The Open leaderboard shortly after he won the playoff, he noted that Andres Romero had finished in third place. He wondered, if only vaguely, how Romero got there before turning his thoughts back to the presentation. Only afterwards did he learn that Romero had the lead when he mounted the 17th tee. "I had absolutely no idea at the time," said Harrington. "It just goes to show how I was in the right place, mentally."

Seven shots behind Sergio Garcia going into the last day, Romero had come bounding through the field with a total of 10 birdies. After making four of those birdies in a row from the 13th, he was leading The Open by two strokes.

Romero's drive on the 17th finished in wispy grass but it was lying well enough. Certainly, there was no cause for alarm. However, when he came to play his second, he was caught between clubs—was it a two iron or was it a three wood? He took the two iron and, seconds later, was watching in mingled horror and disbelief as his golf ball bounced from the stone wall of the Barry Burn into out-of-bounds territory. Once it had been established that there was no mistake, he then hit what was his fourth shot—a three-wood—to the front of the green en route to the double-bogey 6 which had him coming back to the field.

Shock played its part in the bogey Romero notched at the 18th for 67, a score which would leave him one tantalising shot away from the playoff. "I was aware I was leading," Romero said. "I feel very pleased, but the pressure certainly caught up with me, the pressure on the last two holes in such a big event."

The question everyone wanted to ask Romero when he had finished was why, when he had been two ahead, he had not played safe with his second to 17. "I never considered playing safe," he said. "The lie of the ball wasn't bad enough for me to take that decision. I thought I had a chance to get it on the green. I should have hit the three wood and stuck with my initial thought. I didn't, and that was the result.

"I hit a great drive on 18. I hit a poor second shot, but in spite of it all, I'm delighted."

Romero, 26 years of age and from Argentina, had won on the Challenge Tour in 2005 and had three earlier victories in South America. He qualified for his first Open in 2006 and provided a surprise at Hoylake by securing a share of eighth place. "Last year I had the chance of getting myself into this tournament," he said, "and I've certainly thoroughly enjoyed my experience playing this year, and I look forward to next year.

"I am happy," Romero concluded. "The best players in the world were here, and I played in the tournament, and I played with the No 2 in the world (Jim Furyk). I felt very comfortable playing with him and felt I belonged here."

The Sunday after Carnoustie, when news came that Romero had won in Germany, many no doubt were transported back to Johnny Miller's 1976 Open triumph at Royal Birkdale. That was the year the then-unproven Seve Ballesteros finished in a tie for second before going on to do as Romero did, winning his first European Tour event the following week.

—**Lewine Mair**

two double bogeys. "Certainly the pressure caught up with me," he admitted. "But overall I am happy to be playing like this with the best players in the world."

And so the attention returned to Garcia and Harrington. The Irishman parred the 12th and the 13th, but then eagled the 14th, his second shot trickling down the bank on the left onto the green and giving him a 15-footer. He holed it and went to nine under. "Nothing had happened during the round to suggest it was my day until then," Harrington said. "That was a big break."

Behind, Garcia responded. He birdied the 13th from 10 feet and then the 14th, his three-iron approach sailing over to the fourth hole portion of the double green, but the 4 secured with two confident

A round of 70 left Tiger Woods with a share of 12th place.

putts. Ahead, Harrington parred the 15th and the 16th, although at the latter he hit a wonderful tee shot and missed from six feet. A par at 17 and he stood on the final tee one ahead after Garcia had bogeyed the 15th, the result of a poor tee shot.

So Harrington stood on the final tee with driver in hand, just like Van de Velde. It was a poor swing, the ball pushed to the right, and although it tried its best to cross a bridge over the Barry Burn in front of the 17th tee, it slipped off into the water. As Harrington

Harrington hit into the burn with a five iron on his third shot.

For his fifth shot on the 72nd hole, Harrington had a pitch of 47 yards—just like those he practised in his back garden.

Low Scores

Low First Nine
Richard Green   32

Low Second Nine
Hunter Mahan   31

Low Round
Richard Green   64

assessed his position, Garcia, having saved par at the 16th after putting from off the green, passed him on the bridge. He said, "Hello," and smiled. "I just nodded," Harrington recalled. "I couldn't get the words out."

Harrington dropped and took out a five iron. Unlike Van de Velde, who from a similar position had headed right towards the grandstand with unfortunate but disastrous consequences, Harrington took aim at the bunker on the left of the green. He had 207 yards to the front of the green. He was not thinking about the Barry Burn, which crosses just in front of the green, but he should have been. It was another poor shot and he found the water again.

"I was trying to get about 10 yards on the green," he explained. "I was aiming at the out of bounds on the left in a right-to-left wind and trying to cut it in there. It was a difficult shot to take on and I hit a poor shot. I didn't execute well. I hit it fat. I paid the penalty not just for going in the burn with my drive, but being on that side of the fairway and having to play that shot."

When under the severest pressure, Harrington's eyes tend to stick

Garcia could not believe his fate when his putt for par on No 18 lipped out.

out as if on stalks. Briefly there may have been a manic look, but he was fully aware of needing to avoid a Van de Velde-like meltdown. "I didn't want to take 7," he said. "It crossed my mind he had made 7 to lose The Open and I was slipping down that slippery slope." His one advantage was that he had a pitch shot of 47 yards and almost exactly the one he plays in his back garden every day. "I could have hit a pitch-and-run, but I knew the shot I wanted to play. If there is a shot where practice pays off, that was it."

He took the aerial route and the ball checked up on cue five feet past the hole. "It was a lovely pitch, but the putt was the most pressure-filled I had all day," he said. "To hole it was a great boost. That was the moment I thought maybe things are going my way." His son Patrick ran out to meet him as he walked off the green, but sitting in the recorder's hut, watching the television with the sound

"The 18th at Carnoustie is the cruellest hole in golf. The 499-yard par-4 shatters hearts, and careers."

—**Ed Sherman,** *Chicago Tribune*

"Somewhere in France, Jean Van de Velde had to be watching his television, merlot in his glass and a sense of acquittal in his heart. 'This hole is not easy. It is as I tried to tell you,' Van de Velde may have said aloud for anyone to hear."

—**Jim McCabe,** *The Boston Globe*

"Anywhere else, Padraig Harrington might have walked off the 18th green knowing his two shots that found the bottom of the Barry Burn for double bogey had cost him The Open. Not at Carnoustie, where calamity can strike at any second and did in Sunday's final round."

—**Doug Ferguson,**
The Associated Press

"Losing The Open wasn't easy for Sergio Garcia. Now comes the really hard part. Dealing with it."

—**Bob Harig,** *St. Petersburg Times*

"The bridges Padraig Harrington crossed at Carnoustie were six decades long and eight years wide. Ireland has waited since Fred Daly's solitary win at Hoylake in 1947 for a prince to come and lift the Claret Jug at The Open Championship."

—**Karl MacGinty,** *Irish Independent*

On No 1, the first playoff hole, Garcia (above) took bogey-5 from the right bunker, and Harrington holed from 10 feet for a birdie.

down, Harrington maintained his focus on what might be ahead. "Taking 6 was my fault. I hit two poor shots. But I took some comfort in getting up and down, and I was really happy with the way I handled myself from then on.

"I never let it cross my mind that I'd just thrown away The Open. I was as disciplined and focused as I could be not to brood, no ifs or buts. Obviously, if it had turned out that I had thrown away The Open, it would have been incredibly hard to take. I would have struggled in the future to compete in those type of situations again because there would have been so many doubts. But in the hut I didn't let that enter my mind. I knew it was a tough hole, the toughest hole in golf to win a tournament on, and it was going to be tough for Sergio to make a par."

Harrington had finished at seven under par, and with Garcia parring the 17th, the Spaniard needed another par to win. He hit an iron off the tee, but then had to wait to play his second shot as both

Carnoustie's Barry Burn

Shining Star Of The Open

Padraig Harrington deserves plaudits for his victory and Sergio Garcia should be given sympathy for losing out after coming so close, but the shining star of The 136th Open was a stretch of water that snakes its way across the course and for golfers is as much of a distraction as is the mermaid that lures sailors on to the rocks.

After the last two hours of The Open, a time when man was pitted against man and both men were pitted against the course, one image in the mind's eye is of Harrington hitting into the Barry Burn with his tee shot and then his third shot (after dropping out under penalty) on the 72nd hole. Another is of the ball of Andres Romero, who almost made the playoff, landing in the burn, ricocheting out, and ending out of bounds.

The events at Carnoustie this year taught us that the Barry Burn is more treacherous than Rae's Creek at Augusta in the United States, more dangerous than the Swilcan Burn at St Andrews, more intimidating than the Suez Canal at Royal St George's, more understated than the lake by the 17th at Valderrama in Spain, more historic than the water

in front of the 10th and 18th holes at The Belfry. The Barry Burn turns Carnoustie from an exceptionally good course into one not to be found anywhere else in the world.

There are other burns in Scotland, other water hazards on courses around the world. On good days most of these twinkle and sparkle in the sun. The Barry Burn never does that. It may be clear enough in parts so that you can see its floor and see green tendrils of moss, but it never sparkles, never dances in the sunshine. It is tidal for one thing, so the water does not have time to dance. It is constantly on the move.

The burn's sides are stepped, so you can walk down into it, as if descending to a watery grave. You cannot do that in the Suez Canal at Sandwich. It is too wide to try to hurdle, as people do to the Swilcan Burn. And it is never prettied up for special occasions. The idea that the Barry Burn could have blue dye poured into it to make it look better on television, as sometimes happens to the pond that feeds Rae's Creek, would be as heretical to a Scot as adding ice to Glenmorangie.

The Barry Burn neatly symbolises the difference in character and approach between the US and Britain. The 17th at Sawgrass,

the one with a near-island green, is a gimmick, a golf hole by Walt Disney. The Barry Burn at Carnoustie is defined by nature. The water around the penultimate hole at The Players Championship is barely 20 years old, the burn in Scotland is a millennium or more.

The hole in Florida is big, loud, and brash, beating its chest, saying: "Look at me." The burn in Scotland is quiet and sinuous, subtle and seductive.

Darren Clarke described playing the 17th at Sawgrass as waking up in the morning knowing that you have root canal work to be done by your dentist. The Barry Burn has a similar effect. "There wasn't a competitor in The Open last week who didn't find it was preying on his mind all the way round," Martin Kippax, the Chairman of the Championship Committee, said. "You know it is waiting."

The Barry Burn was there for Carnoustie's first Open in 1931, creating anxiety, wreaking havoc, and it will be there for ever more.

—John Hopkins

---

bunkers around the green had to be raked after the group in front had finished. Garcia pulled his three-iron approach into the bunker on the left and was later annoyed about the wait. The recovery came out to 10 feet, and though the putt appeared to be curving into the hole, it hit the left side of the cup and stayed out. Garcia had closed with a 73 to Harrington's 67 and the pair were tied on 277, seven under. It was the third Open in a row at Carnoustie to go to a playoff.

Paul McGinley was watching in the Irish corner, Miguel Angel Jimenez in the Spanish corner, both relieved Europe would have its first major champion since Lawrie. The vital action was at the first and involved Garcia finding the front right bunker with his approach, and taking a bogey, while Harrington holed from 10 feet for a birdie. Garcia hit the flagstick at the 16th, but the ball spun

Championship Totals	
Players Below Par	88
Players At Par	40
Players Above Par	324

Victory Eludes Garcia Again

'I'm still asking myself, trying to find an answer.'

After exuding remarkable control for three days, there was something emotional about Sergio Garcia when he returned to the first tee on Sunday afternoon. Even though he held a three-shot lead over Steve Stricker and was six strokes ahead of the rest, the calm assurance of the first three rounds seemed to have vanished.

As the putts declined to drop and chips were fluffed, Garcia struggled over the outward nine to cope with the pressure of leading from the front in a major championship.

The anxieties attached to winning a first major gnaw at the souls of those seeking victory. Garcia looked like a man who had slept fitfully, even though the warmth of the galleries who lined the fairways at Carnoustie must have reminded the 27-year-old that he was a crowd favourite as well as the bookmakers' favourite to triumph.

Two over par for the day by the turn, Garcia fell even further behind on the 13th tee when he trailed the lead by two shots. It was at this point a man unsure whether to attack or defend the links was left with no option but to make a move. He made birdies on the 13th and 14th holes, and even the shot dropped on the 15th was due to ambition rather than inhibition.

With a chance to hoist the Claret Jug if he made 4, a par on the last, however, the Spaniard put the emphasis on safety off the tee by using a two iron for position. It left the Spaniard with a brutally difficult second shot with a three iron. When he was bunkered and narrowly failed from 10 feet to get up and down, Garcia's closing 73 handed Padraig Harrington the reprieve of victory in a playoff.

"I definitely struggled on the front nine," Garcia said. "I had my opportunities. Unfortunately I didn't convert ... I hit some good shots coming in. It's just one of those things ... I still don't know how that par putt missed. I'm still asking myself, trying to find an answer on that.

"And then, I don't know. I should write a book on how not to miss a shot in the playoff and shoot one over. It is the way it is. I guess it's not news in my life. I just have to move on and hopefully do better next time."

According to Ryder Cup teammate Colin Montgomerie, Garcia will bounce back. "I think he'll handle it quite well," said the Scot. "Sergio is good enough and young enough to come back. The putts just didn't go in during the last round."

—Mike Aitken

For the second time, Garcia thought he had holed the putt on No 18, but that was not to be.

away to 18 feet, although it would probably have been farther without the interference. Still, afterwards, in his bitter disappointment, Garcia saw it as a misfortune too far.

Harrington was off the green to the left, but, with the perfect touch he displayed on the delicate shots all week, he putted up and tapped in. A par each and the 17th was halved in pars as well. Harrington was two ahead going to the last and would like to have been three ahead. He chose the safe route, taking a hybrid off the tee and laying up short of the water. "Let's make a 5," was his thinking. "It seemed sensible to put the pressure on Sergio and make him make a 3. If he does, then I'd slap him on the back, say well done, and know we would be going on."

Needing something to happen, Garcia went with the driver off the tee and it found the left rough. But he had a shot to the green and produced a terrific six iron to 20 feet. Harrington's third was

A four-foot putt for bogey-5 meant that Harrington had become The Open champion.

on the green but only just. His 30-footer for par was meant as a lag but rolled on just a little farther than ideal. Now if Garcia made birdie, Harrington would need to hole out just to stay alive. For the second time in an hour, Garcia thought he had made his putt, but it whizzed by the edge yet again. He made the one back, forcing Harrington to do likewise, but there was no way back now for the Spaniard.

"It is tough mainly because I don't feel like I did anything wrong," Garcia said afterwards, his disappointment self-evident. "I didn't miss a shot in the playoff and hit unbelievable putts, but they just didn't want to go in. It just wasn't meant to happen. It seems to me that every time I get in this

Garcia was consoled by countryman Jimenez.

Championship Hole Summary

HOLE	PAR	YARDS	EAGLES	BIRDIES	PARS	BOGEYS	D.BOGEYS	HIGHER	RANK	AVERAGE
1	4	406	0	85	317	44	6	0	15	3.94
2	4	463	0	67	276	93	15	1	11	4.13
3	4	358	0	62	261	109	18	2	8	4.20
4	4	412	0	90	320	39	2	1	16	3.90
5	4	415	0	41	252	128	30	1	5	4.33
6	5	578	5	174	190	65	12	6	17	4.83
7	4	410	0	64	316	65	7	0	12	4.03
8	3	183	0	53	300	83	13	3	10	3.14
9	4	478	0	37	292	109	12	2	7	4.23
OUT	36	3703	5	673	2524	735	115	16		36.73
10	4	466	0	36	259	127	26	4	4	4.34
11	4	383	1	79	309	59	4	0	13	3.97
12	4	499	0	21	261	146	22	2	2	4.39
13	3	176	0	84	304	63	1	0	14	2.96
14	5	514	19	210	187	30	4	2	18	4.55
15	4	472	1	25	266	139	18	3	3	4.35
16	3	248	0	19	281	144	8	0	6	3.31
17	4	461	0	34	314	97	7	0	9	4.17
18	4	499	0	17	209	172	44	10	1	4.61
IN	35	3718	21	525	2390	977	134	21		36.65
TOTAL	71	7421	26	1198	4914	1712	249	37		73.38

A family celebration for Padraig, Patrick, and Caroline.

kind of position I have no room for error. But the week is over. Padraig played well today and well enough to win."

An elated Harrington could still empathise with his opponent. "I could see the disappointment of losing for Sergio," he said. "He was under so much pressure to win a major, but he's an incredible talent and probably the best ball striker in the game. He's young and he's going to win a major, he's going to win majors. It's going to happen. The more he believes that, the quicker it will happen."

But it was Harrington who lifted the Claret Jug and addressed the gallery with dignified and heartfelt words. Oblivious to it all was four-year-old Patrick Harrington. His dad had the old trophy, but to him it was just a new plaything. "Daddy, can we put ladybirds in it?" Patrick asked. "We can, indeed," replied The Open champion. "We can, indeed."

A Tale Of Ladybirds And Glass Jaws

By John Hopkins

You gain an insight into the character of Padraig Harrington upon hearing the ladybird story, one that will go down in golfing history. It involves him and Patrick, his four-year-old son. Padraig was holding the Claret Jug after winning the playoff when Patrick ran across to him and looked at the old trophy. Padraig might have wondered what was going to happen next. It did not take long for him to find out. "Can we put ladybirds in it?" Patrick asked with all the innocence of a four-year-old.

Padraig might have said: "Oh, you'd better ask your Mother." Or he might have laughed and tousled his son's head and said: "Get away with you." Instead he gave a serious answer to a serious question, not patronising his son in the least. "We can, indeed. We can, indeed," was his reply.

More than that though is revealed by the relationship between father and son. After Harrington had taken a 6 on the 72nd hole, Caroline, his wife, let Patrick loose to run to his father and jump into his arms. There were no concerns that Padraig might be distracted from preparing for a playoff. There were no concerns about anything, in fact, except the attention of his young son, which may of course, have been just the tonic he needed. At that moment he might instead have thought he had lost The Open. Patrick made sure he did not dwell on it.

Here is one fact you probably didn't know about Harrington, 35 years of age. He drives a 10-year-old Mercedes that has done only 22,000 miles. Extravagant he is not.

Here is another. His favourite book is *The Alchemist* by Paul Coelho, best described as a fable about following your dream towards personal contentment and riches.

And a third. Harrington is fit. Among those who visit the gym and concentrate on improving their core stability, there is an exercise known as the plank. You have to hold yourself a foot or so off the ground resting on your elbows and toes for a minute or two at a time, keeping your body as straight as a plank as you do so. Harrington does this for three minutes—with a 60 kilos weight on his back.

Look at Harrington and you see a man with short dark hair always neatly combed. He looks like the accountant he once was, a man you can easily imagine poring over a balance sheet. He has alert eyes and a way of cocking his head on one side as he listens to what you're saying. Often there is a ready smile on his face. He gives each question full respect. He could never be accused of being parsimonious with his words. Indeed it is sometimes said that if you can follow Harrington's logic when he embarks on one of his long-winded answers then you are more blessed than most.

It is doubtful whether there could have been a more popular winner. Harrington is admired by his peers for his work ethic and highly thought of by the journalists whose role it is to chronicle his successes. Golfers have a right to be protected, to have their private lives kept to themselves, to maintain a distance between them and everyone else. However, Harrington's mobile telephone number may be in the contacts book of more journalists than any other player of that level. He is as uncomplicated to deal with as it is possible to be. There seems to be no side to him. He always seems to be the same whether he has just signed his card incorrectly and been disqualified, whether he is worried about his dying father, or whether he has just gone round in 73.

It is typical of Harrington that he has been taught by only one man for the past dozen years. Let others go off in search of new teachers when their play takes a downturn. Padraig Harrington is a disciple of Bob Torrance who, in turn, is a disciple of Ben Hogan. Harrington likes Torrance because when he does what he is told he plays well. Torrance likes Harrington because he is the only player with whom he has ever worked who is prepared to put in as much time as he is. If you were given a pound for every hour the two men had spent working together on Harrington's game at Largs in Scotland, you would be a rich man. Bob Torrance believes the game starts from the legs up. So does Harrington. "It's no good having arms like Popeye if you have legs like Olive Oyl," Bob Torrance once told a pupil.

How appropriate then that on the eve of the Open at the course where Hogan had triumphed in 1953, Bob Torrance should have been given an award for outstanding services to golf—and that Harrington should have been present to introduce Torrance to the assembled gathering.

Harrington's swing has none of the fluid power of that of Ernie Els nor the raw power of that of Tiger Woods. It looks like a thing that is made up of many moving parts. Yet it is more reliable than it might seem and generates more power than you might think. Most of it all, his swing has made him something of a short game wizard. Think of short game experts and you think of Jose Maria Olazabal and Phil Mickelson, but if you wanted a man to chip for your life, you could do a lot worse than summon Harrington.

He is a family man to his boots, and he and Caroline often exemplify the saying that two people can have the strength of three. Caroline Harrington is a powerful force for the good in this relationship. She once told an interviewer: "Padraig hasn't seen a credit card bill or any kind of a bill since the day we got together." She told the same interviewer: "If you left the booking of restaurants to Padraig, we'd all starve."

Before Carnoustie Harrington had come second in 30 tournaments. Again and again it seemed that just when he could have won a tournament, indeed should have, he failed to do so. He referred to this in his hour of triumph when he said that if he had lost the playoff he would have given the game up. This should be taken with a pinch of salt, but you get his gist.

The following conversation between an Irishman and a journalist took place at Carnoustie on the eve of the Championship.

"So who do you think will win?" the Irishman asked.

"Other than Woods, you mean?"

"How about Harrington?"

"Bit worried that he has come second so many times. He might have a glass jaw."

The two men met by chance on Monday morning.

"Good old Paddy," said Barry the Irishman. Then he added, impishly: "Pity about the glass jaw."

The Open Championship Results

Year	Champion	Score	Margin	Runners-up	Venue
1860	Willie Park Snr	174	2	Tom Morris Snr	Prestwick
1861	Tom Morris Snr	163	4	Willie Park Snr	Prestwick
1862	Tom Morris Snr	163	13	Willie Park Snr	Prestwick
1863	Willie Park Snr	168	2	Tom Morris Snr	Prestwick
1864	Tom Morris Snr	167	2	Andrew Strath	Prestwick
1865	Andrew Strath	162	2	Willie Park Snr	Prestwick
1866	Willie Park Snr	169	2	David Park	Prestwick
1867	Tom Morris Snr	170	2	Willie Park Snr	Prestwick
1868	Tom Morris Jnr	154	3	Tom Morris Snr	Prestwick
1869	Tom Morris Jnr	157	11	Bob Kirk	Prestwick
1870	Tom Morris Jnr	149	12	Bob Kirk, David Strath	Prestwick
1871	*No Competition*				
1872	Tom Morris Jnr	166	3	David Strath	Prestwick
1873	Tom Kidd	179	1	Jamie Anderson	St Andrews
1874	Mungo Park	159	2	Tom Morris Jnr	Musselburgh
1875	Willie Park Snr	166	2	Bob Martin	Prestwick
1876	Bob Martin	176	—	David Strath	St Andrews
	(Martin was awarded the title when Strath refused to play-off)				
1877	Jamie Anderson	160	2	Bob Pringle	Musselburgh
1878	Jamie Anderson	157	2	Bob Kirk	Prestwick
1879	Jamie Anderson	169	3	James Allan, Andrew Kirkaldy	St Andrews
1880	Bob Ferguson	162	5	Peter Paxton	Musselburgh
1881	Bob Ferguson	170	3	Jamie Anderson	Prestwick
1882	Bob Ferguson	171	3	Willie Fernie	St Andrews
1883	Willie Fernie	158	Playoff	Bob Ferguson	Musselburgh
1884	Jack Simpson	160	4	Douglas Rolland, Willie Fernie	Prestwick
1885	Bob Martin	171	1	Archie Simpson	St Andrews
1886	David Brown	157	2	Willie Campbell	Musselburgh
1887	Willie Park Jnr	161	1	Bob Martin	Prestwick
1888	Jack Burns	171	1	David Anderson Jnr, Ben Sayers	St Andrews
1889	Willie Park Jnr	155	Playoff	Andrew Kirkaldy	Musselburgh
1890	John Ball Jnr*	164	3	Willie Fernie, Archie Simpson	Prestwick
1891	Hugh Kirkaldy	166	2	Willie Fernie, Andrew Kirkaldy	St Andrews

(From 1892 the competition was extended to 72 holes)

Year	Champion	Score	Margin	Runners-up	Venue
1892	Harold Hilton*	305	3	John Ball Jnr*, Hugh Kirkaldy, Sandy Herd	Muirfield

Tony Jacklin (1969)

Sandy Lyle (1985)

Year	Champion	Score	Margin	Runners-up	Venue
1893	Willie Auchterlonie	322	2	John Laidlay*	Prestwick
1894	J H Taylor	326	5	Douglas Rolland	Sandwich
1895	J H Taylor	322	4	Sandy Herd	St Andrews
1896	Harry Vardon	316	Playoff	J H Taylor	Muirfield
1897	Harold Hilton*	314	1	James Braid	Hoylake
1898	Harry Vardon	307	1	Willie Park Jnr	Prestwick
1899	Harry Vardon	310	5	Jack White	Sandwich
1900	J H Taylor	309	8	Harry Vardon	St Andrews
1901	James Braid	309	3	Harry Vardon	Muirfield
1902	Sandy Herd	307	1	Harry Vardon, James Braid	Hoylake
1903	Harry Vardon	300	6	Tom Vardon	Prestwick
1904	Jack White	296	1	James Braid, J H Taylor	Sandwich
1905	James Braid	318	5	J H Taylor, Rowland Jones	St Andrews
1906	James Braid	300	4	J H Taylor	Muirfield
1907	Arnaud Massy	312	2	J H Taylor	Hoylake
1908	James Braid	291	8	Tom Ball	Prestwick
1909	J H Taylor	295	6	James Braid, Tom Ball	Deal
1910	James Braid	299	4	Sandy Herd	St Andrews
1911	Harry Vardon	303	Playoff	Arnaud Massy	Sandwich
1912	Ted Ray	295	4	Harry Vardon	Muirfield
1913	J H Taylor	304	8	Ted Ray	Hoylake
1914	Harry Vardon	306	3	J H Taylor	Prestwick
1915-1919	*No Championship*				
1920	George Duncan	303	2	Sandy Herd	Deal
1921	Jock Hutchison	296	Playoff	Roger Wethered*	St Andrews
1922	Walter Hagen	300	1	George Duncan, Jim Barnes	Sandwich
1923	Arthur G Havers	295	1	Walter Hagen	Troon
1924	Walter Hagen	301	1	Ernest Whitcombe	Hoylake
1925	Jim Barnes	300	1	Archie Compston, Ted Ray	Prestwick
1926	Robert T Jones Jnr*	291	2	Al Watrous	Royal Lytham
1927	Robert T Jones Jnr*	285	6	Aubrey Boomer, Fred Robson	St Andrews
1928	Walter Hagen	292	2	Gene Sarazen	Sandwich
1929	Walter Hagen	292	6	John Farrell	Muirfield
1930	Robert T Jones Jnr*	291	2	Leo Diegel, Macdonald Smith	Hoylake

Year	Champion	Score	Margin	Runners-up	Venue
1931	Tommy Armour	296	1	Jose Jurado	Carnoustie
1932	Gene Sarazen	283	5	Macdonald Smith	Prince's
1933	Densmore Shute	292	Playoff	Craig Wood	St Andrews
1934	Henry Cotton	283	5	Sid Brews	Sandwich
1935	Alf Perry	283	4	Alf Padgham	Muirfield
1936	Alf Padgham	287	1	Jimmy Adams	Hoylake
1937	Henry Cotton	290	2	Reg Whitcombe	Carnoustie
1938	Reg Whitcombe	295	2	Jimmy Adams	Sandwich
1939	Richard Burton	290	2	Johnny Bulla	St Andrews
1940-1945 *No Championship*					
1946	Sam Snead	290	4	Bobby Locke, Johnny Bulla	St Andrews
1947	Fred Daly	293	1	Reg Horne, Frank Stranahan*	Hoylake
1948	Henry Cotton	284	5	Fred Daly	Muirfield
1949	Bobby Locke	283	Playoff	Harry Bradshaw	Sandwich
1950	Bobby Locke	279	2	Roberto de Vicenzo	Troon
1951	Max Faulkner	285	2	Tony Cerda	Royal Portrush
1952	Bobby Locke	287	1	Peter Thomson	Royal Lytham
1953	Ben Hogan	282	4	Frank Stranahan*, Dai Rees, Peter Thomson, Tony Cerda	Carnoustie
1954	Peter Thomson	283	1	Sid Scott, Dai Rees, Bobby Locke	Royal Birkdale
1955	Peter Thomson	281	2	Johnny Fallon	St Andrews
1956	Peter Thomson	286	3	Flory van Donck	Hoylake
1957	Bobby Locke	279	3	Peter Thomson	St Andrews
1958	Peter Thomson	278	Playoff	David Thomas	Royal Lytham
1959	Gary Player	284	2	Flory van Donck, Fred Bullock	Muirfield
1960	Kel Nagle	278	1	Arnold Palmer	St Andrews
1961	Arnold Palmer	284	1	Dai Rees	Royal Birkdale
1962	Arnold Palmer	276	6	Kel Nagle	Troon
1963	Bob Charles	277	Playoff	Phil Rodgers	Royal Lytham
1964	Tony Lema	279	5	Jack Nicklaus	St Andrews
1965	Peter Thomson	285	2	Christy O'Connor, Brian Huggett	Royal Birkdale
1966	Jack Nicklaus	282	1	David Thomas, Doug Sanders	Muirfield
1967	Roberto de Vicenzo	278	2	Jack Nicklaus	Hoylake
1968	Gary Player	289	2	Jack Nicklaus, Bob Charles	Carnoustie
1969	Tony Jacklin	280	2	Bob Charles	Royal Lytham
1970	Jack Nicklaus	283	Playoff	Doug Sanders	St Andrews

Ben Curtis (2003)

John Daly (1995)

Todd Hamilton (2004)

Paul Lawrie (1999)

Year	Champion	Score	Margin	Runners-up	Venue
1971	Lee Trevino	278	1	Lu Liang Huan	Royal Birkdale
1972	Lee Trevino	278	1	Jack Nicklaus	Muirfield
1973	Tom Weiskopf	276	3	Neil Coles, Johnny Miller	Troon
1974	Gary Player	282	4	Peter Oosterhuis	Royal Lytham
1975	Tom Watson	279	Playoff	Jack Newton	Carnoustie
1976	Johnny Miller	279	6	Jack Nicklaus, Severiano Ballesteros	Royal Birkdale
1977	Tom Watson	268	1	Jack Nicklaus	Turnberry
1978	Jack Nicklaus	281	2	Simon Owen, Ben Crenshaw, Raymond Floyd, Tom Kite	St Andrews
1979	Severiano Ballesteros	283	3	Jack Nicklaus, Ben Crenshaw	Royal Lytham
1980	Tom Watson	271	4	Lee Trevino	Muirfield
1981	Bill Rogers	276	4	Bernhard Langer	Sandwich
1982	Tom Watson	284	1	Peter Oosterhuis, Nick Price	Royal Troon
1983	Tom Watson	275	1	Hale Irwin, Andy Bean	Royal Birkdale
1984	Severiano Ballesteros	276	2	Bernhard Langer, Tom Watson	St Andrews
1985	Sandy Lyle	282	1	Payne Stewart	Sandwich
1986	Greg Norman	280	5	Gordon J. Brand	Turnberry
1987	Nick Faldo	279	1	Rodger Davis, Paul Azinger	Muirfield
1988	Severiano Ballesteros	273	2	Nick Price	Royal Lytham
1989	Mark Calcavecchia	275	Playoff	Greg Norman, Wayne Grady	Royal Troon
1990	Nick Faldo	270	5	Mark McNulty, Payne Stewart	St Andrews
1991	Ian Baker-Finch	272	2	Mike Harwood	Royal Birkdale
1992	Nick Faldo	272	1	John Cook	Muirfield
1993	Greg Norman	267	2	Nick Faldo	Sandwich
1994	Nick Price	268	1	Jesper Parnevik	Turnberry
1995	John Daly	282	Playoff	Costantino Rocca	St Andrews
1996	Tom Lehman	271	2	Mark McCumber, Ernie Els	Royal Lytham
1997	Justin Leonard	272	3	Jesper Parnevik, Darren Clarke	Royal Troon
1998	Mark O'Meara	280	Playoff	Brian Watts	Royal Birkdale
1999	Paul Lawrie	290	Playoff	Justin Leonard, Jean Van de Velde	Carnoustie
2000	Tiger Woods	269	8	Ernie Els, Thomas Bjorn	St Andrews
2001	David Duval	274	3	Niclas Fasth	Royal Lytham
2002	Ernie Els	278	Playoff	Thomas Levet, Stuart Appleby, Steve Elkington	Muirfield
2003	Ben Curtis	283	1	Thomas Bjorn, Vijay Singh	Sandwich
2004	Todd Hamilton	274	Playoff	Ernie Els	Royal Troon
2005	Tiger Woods	274	5	Colin Montgomerie	St Andrews
2006	Tiger Woods	270	2	Chris DiMarco	Hoylake
2007	Padraig Harrington	277	Playoff	Sergio Garcia	Carnoustie

*Denotes amateurs

The Open Championship Records

Most Victories

6, Harry Vardon, 1896-98-99-1903-11-14
5, James Braid, 1901-05-06-08-10; J H Taylor, 1894-95-1900-09-13; Peter Thomson, 1954-55-56-58-65; Tom Watson, 1975-77-80-82-83

Most Times Runner-Up or Joint Runner-Up

7, Jack Nicklaus, 1964-67-68-72-76-77-79
6, J H Taylor, 1896-1904-05-06-07-14

Oldest Winner

Old Tom Morris, 46 years 99 days, 1867
Harry Vardon, 44 years 41 days, 1914
Roberto de Vicenzo, 44 years 93 days, 1967

Youngest Winner

Young Tom Morris, 17 years 5 months 3 days, 1868
Willie Auchterlonie, 21 years 24 days, 1893
Severiano Ballesteros, 22 years 3 months 12 days, 1979

Youngest and Oldest Competitor

Young Tom Morris, 14 years 4 months 25 days, 1865
Gene Sarazen, 74 years 4 months 9 days, 1976

Justin Leonard (1997)

Biggest Margin of Victory

13 strokes, Old Tom Morris, 1862
12 strokes, Young Tom Morris, 1870
11 strokes, Young Tom Morris, 1869
8 strokes, J H Taylor, 1900 and 1913; James Braid, 1908; Tiger Woods, 2000

Lowest Winning Aggregates

267 (66, 68, 69, 64), Greg Norman, Royal St George's, 1993
268 (68, 70, 65, 65), Tom Watson, Turnberry, 1977; (69, 66, 67, 66), Nick Price, Turnberry, 1994
269 (67, 66, 67, 69), Tiger Woods, St Andrews, 2000

Lowest Aggregates in Relation to Par

269 (19 under par), Tiger Woods, St Andrews, 2000
270 (18 under par), Nick Faldo, St Andrews, 1990; Tiger Woods, Hoylake, 2006

Lowest Aggregates by Runner-Up

269 (68, 70, 65, 66), Jack Nicklaus, Turnberry, 1977; (69, 63, 70, 67), Nick Faldo, Royal St George's, 1993; (68, 66, 68, 67), Jesper Parnevik, Turnberry, 1994

Lowest Aggregates by an Amateur

281 (68, 72, 70, 71), Iain Pyman, Royal St George's, 1993; (75, 66, 70, 70), Tiger Woods, Royal Lytham, 1996

Lowest Individual Round

63, Mark Hayes, second round, Turnberry, 1977; Isao Aoki, third round, Muirfield, 1980; Greg Norman, second round, Turnberry, 1986; Paul Broadhurst, third round, St Andrews, 1990; Jodie Mudd, fourth round, Royal Birkdale, 1991; Nick Faldo, second round, and Payne Stewart, fourth round, Royal St George's, 1993

Lowest Individual Round by an Amateur

66, Frank Stranahan, fourth round, Troon, 1950; Tiger Woods, second round, Royal Lytham, 1996; Justin Rose, second round, Royal Birkdale, 1998

Tiger Woods (2000, 2005, 2006)

Lowest First Round

64, Craig Stadler, Royal Birkdale, 1983; Christy O'Connor Jnr, Royal St George's, 1985; Rodger Davis, Muirfield, 1987; Raymond Floyd and Steve Pate, Muirfield, 1992

Lowest Second Round

63, Mark Hayes, Turnberry, 1977; Greg Norman, Turnberry, 1986; Nick Faldo, Royal St George's, 1993

Lowest Third Round

63, Isao Aoki, Muirfield, 1980; Paul Broadhurst, St Andrews, 1990

Lowest Fourth Round

63, Jodie Mudd, Royal Birkdale, 1991; Payne Stewart, Royal St George's, 1993

Lowest First 36 Holes

130 (66, 64), Nick Faldo, Muirfield, 1992

Lowest Second 36 Holes

130 (65, 65), Tom Watson, Turnberry, 1977; (64, 66), Ian Baker-Finch, Royal Birkdale, 1991; (66, 64), Anders Forsbrand, Turnberry, 1994

Lowest Middle 36 Holes

130 (66, 64), Fuzzy Zoeller, Turnberry, 1994

Lowest First 54 Holes

198 (67, 67, 64), Tom Lehman, Royal Lytham, 1996
199 (67, 65, 67), Nick Faldo, St Andrews, 1990; (66, 64, 69), Nick Faldo, Muirfield, 1992

Lowest Final 54 Holes

199 (66, 67, 66), Nick Price, Turnberry, 1994

Lowest 9 Holes

28, Denis Durnian, first 9, Royal Birkdale, 1983
29, Peter Thomson and Tom Haliburton, first 9, Royal Lytham, 1958; Tony Jacklin, first 9, St Andrews, 1970; Bill Longmuir, first 9, Royal Lytham, 1979; David J Russell, first 9, Royal Lytham, 1988; Ian Baker-Finch and Paul Broadhurst, St Andrews, 1990; Ian Baker-Finch, first 9, Royal Birkdale, 1991; Paul McGinley, first 9, Royal Lytham, 1996; Ernie Els, first 9, Muirfield, 2002; Sergio Garcia, first 9, Royal Liverpool, 2006

Successive Victories

4, Young Tom Morris, 1868-72 (no Championship in 1871)
3, Jamie Anderson, 1877-79; Bob Ferguson, 1880-82, Peter Thomson, 1954-56
2, Old Tom Morris, 1861-62; J H Taylor, 1894-95; Harry Vardon, 1898-99; James Braid, 1905-06; Bobby Jones, 1926-27; Walter Hagen, 1928-29; Bobby Locke, 1949-50; Arnold Palmer, 1961-62; Lee Trevino, 1971-72; Tom Watson, 1982-83; Tiger Woods, 2005-06

Victories by Amateurs

3, Bobby Jones, 1926-27-30
2, Harold Hilton, 1892-97
1, John Ball, 1890
Roger Wethered lost a playoff in 1921

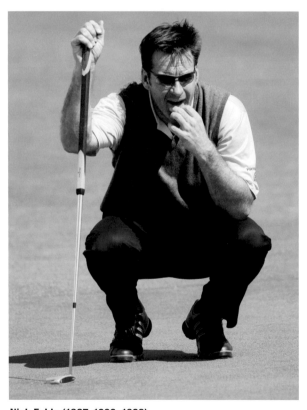

Nick Faldo (1987, 1990, 1992)

Mark O'Meara (1998)

Tom Lehman (1996)

Champions in First Appearance

Willie Park, Prestwick, 1860; Tom Kidd, St Andrews, 1873; Mungo Park, Musselburgh, 1874; Harold Hilton, Muirfield, 1892; Jock Hutchison, St Andrews, 1921; Densmore Shute, St Andrews, 1933; Ben Hogan, Carnoustie, 1953; Tony Lema, St Andrews, 1964; Tom Watson, Carnoustie, 1975; Ben Curtis, Sandwich, 2003

Biggest Span Between First and Last Victories

19 years, J H Taylor, 1894-1913
18 years, Harry Vardon, 1896-1914
15 years, Gary Player, 1959-74
14 years, Willie Park Snr, 1860-75 (no competition 1871); Henry Cotton, 1934-48

Biggest Span Between Victories

11 years, Henry Cotton, 1937-48

Champions in Three Decades

Harry Vardon, 1896, 1903, 1911
J H Taylor, 1894, 1900, 1913
Gary Player, 1959, 1968, 1974

Highest Number of Top-Five Finishes

16, J H Taylor, Jack Nicklaus
15, Harry Vardon, James Braid

Highest Number of Rounds Under Par

61, Jack Nicklaus
52, Nick Faldo
44, Tom Watson

Highest Number of Aggregates Under Par

14, Jack Nicklaus, Nick Faldo

Most Consecutive Rounds Under 70

7, Ernie Els, 1993-94

Outright Leader After Every Round

Ted Ray, 1912; Bobby Jones, 1927; Gene Sarazen, 1932; Henry Cotton, 1934; Tom Weiskopf, 1973; Tiger Woods, 2005

Leader After Every Round Including Ties

Harry Vardon, 1899 and 1903; J H Taylor, 1900; Lee Trevino, 1971; Gary Player, 1974

Record Leads (Since 1892)

After 18 holes:
4 strokes, James Braid, 1908; Bobby Jones, 1927; Henry Cotton, 1934; Christy O'Connor Jnr, 1985
After 36 holes:
9 strokes, Henry Cotton, 1934
After 54 holes:
10 strokes, Henry Cotton, 1934
7 strokes, Tony Lema, 1964

Biggest Leads by Non-Champions

After 54 holes:
5 strokes, Macdonald Smith, 1925; Jean Van de Velde, 1999

Champions with Each Round Lower Than Previous One

Jack White, 1904, Sandwich, (80, 75, 72, 69)
James Braid, 1906, Muirfield, (77, 76, 74, 73)
Henry Cotton, 1937, Carnoustie, (74, 73, 72, 71)
Ben Hogan, 1953, Carnoustie, (73, 71, 70, 68)
Gary Player, 1959, Muirfield, (75, 71, 70, 68)

Champion with Four Rounds the Same

Densmore Shute, 1933, St Andrews, (73, 73, 73, 73) (excluding the playoff)

Biggest Variation Between Rounds of a Champion

14 strokes, Henry Cotton, 1934, second round 65, fourth round 79
11 strokes, Jack White, 1904, first round 80, fourth round 69; Greg Norman, 1986, first round 74, second round 63, third round 74

Biggest Variation Between Two Rounds

20 strokes, R G French, 1938, second round 71, third round 91; Colin Montgomerie, 2002, second round 64, third round 84
19 strokes, R H Pemberton, 1938, second round 72, third round 91
18 strokes, A Tingey Jnr, 1923, first round 94, second round 76
17 strokes, Jack Nicklaus, 1981, first round 83, second round 66; Ian Baker-Finch, 1986, first round 86, second round 69

Best Comeback by Champions

After 18 holes:
Harry Vardon, 1896, 11 strokes behind the leader
After 36 holes:
George Duncan, 1920, 13 strokes behind the leader
After 54 holes:
Paul Lawrie, 1999, 10 strokes behind the leader

Champions with Four Rounds Under 70

Greg Norman, 1993, Royal St George's, (66, 68, 69, 64); Nick Price, 1994, Turnberry, (69, 66, 67, 66); Tiger Woods, 2000, St Andrews, (67, 66, 67, 69)
Of non-champions:
Ernie Els, 1993, Royal St George's, (68, 69, 69, 68); Jesper Parnevik, 1994, Turnberry, (68, 66, 68, 67); Ernie Els, 2004, Royal Troon, (69, 69, 68, 68)

Best Finishing Round by a Champion

64, Greg Norman, Royal St George's, 1993
65, Tom Watson, Turnberry, 1977; Severiano Ballesteros, Royal Lytham, 1988; Justin Leonard, Royal Troon, 1997

Worst Round by a Champion Since 1939

78, Fred Daly, third round, Hoylake, 1947
76, Paul Lawrie, third round, Carnoustie, 1999

Worst Finishing Round by a Champion Since 1939

75, Sam Snead, St Andrews, 1946

Best Opening Round by a Champion

66, Peter Thomson, Royal Lytham, 1958; Nick Faldo, Muirfield, 1992; Greg Norman, Royal St George's, 1993; Tiger Woods, St Andrews, 2005

Biggest Recovery in 18 Holes by a Champion

George Duncan, Deal, 1920, was 13 strokes behind the leader, Abe Mitchell, after 36 holes and level after 54

Most Appearances

46, Gary Player
38, Jack Nicklaus

Ernie Els (2002)

Most Appearances on Final Day (Since 1892)

32, Jack Nicklaus
31, Alex Herd
30, J H Taylor
27, Harry Vardon, James Braid, Nick Faldo
26, Peter Thomson, Gary Player
23, Dai Rees
22, Henry Cotton

Most Appearances Before First Victory

16, Nick Price, 1994
14, Mark O'Meara, 1998

Most Appearances Without a Victory

29, Dai Rees
28, Sam Torrance
27, Neil Coles

Championship with Highest Number of Rounds Under 70

148, Turnberry, 1994

Championship Since 1946 with the Fewest Rounds Under 70

St Andrews, 1946; Hoylake, 1947; Portrush, 1951; Hoylake, 1956; Carnoustie, 1968. All had only two rounds under 70.

Longest Course

Carnoustie, 2007, 7421 yards

Courses Most Often Used

St Andrews, 27; Prestwick, 24; Muirfield, 15; Sandwich, 13; Hoylake, 11; Royal Lytham, 10; Royal Birkdale and Royal Troon, 8; Carnoustie, 7; Musselburgh, 6; Turnberry, 3; Deal, 2; Royal Portrush and Prince's, 1

Prize Money

Year	Total	First Prize
1860	nil	nil
1863	10	nil
1864	15	6
1876	27	10
1889	22	8
1891	30.50	10
1892	100	35
1893	100	30
1910	135	50
1920	225	75
1927	275	75
1930	400	100
1931	500	100
1946	1,000	150
1949	1,500	300
1953	2,500	500
1954	3,500	750
1955	3,750	1,000
1958	4,850	1,000
1959	5,000	1,000
1960	7,000	1,250
1961	8,500	1,400
1963	8,500	1,500
1965	10,000	1,750
1966	15,000	2,100
1968	20,000	3,000
1969	30,334	4,250
1970	40,000	5,250
1971	45,000	5,500
1972	50,000	5,500
1975	75,000	7,500
1977	100,000	10,000
1978	125,000	12,500
1979	155,000	15,000
1980	200,000	25,000
1982	250,000	32,000
1983	310,000	40,000
1984	445,000	50,000
1985	530,000	65,000
1986	634,000	70,000
1987	650,000	75,000
1988	700,000	80,000
1989	750,000	80,000
1990	825,000	85,000

Year	Total	First Prize
1991	900,000	90,000
1992	950,000	95,000
1993	1,000,000	100,000
1994	1,100,000	110,000
1995	1,250,000	125,000
1996	1,400,000	200,000
1997	1,586,300	250,000
1998	1,800,000	300,000
1999	2,000,000	350,000

Year	Total	First Prize
2000	2,750,000	500,000
2001	3,300,000	600,000
2002	3,800,000	700,000
2003	3,900,000	700,000
2004	4,000,000	720,000
2005	4,000,000	720,000
2006	4,000,000	720,000
2007	4,200,000	750,000

Attendance

Year	Total	Year	Total	Year	Total
1962	37,098	1978	125,271	1993	141,000
1963	24,585	1979	134,501	1994	128,000
1964	35,954			1995	180,000
1965	32,927	1980	131,610	1996	170,000
1966	40,182	1981	111,987	1997	176,000
1967	29,880	1982	133,299	1998	195,100
1968	51,819	1983	142,892	1999	157,000
1969	46,001	1984	193,126		
		1985	141,619	2000	238,787
1970	81,593	1986	134,261	2001	178,000
1971	70,076	1987	139,189	2002	161,500
1972	84,746	1988	191,334	2003	183,000
1973	78,810	1989	160,639	2004	176,000
1974	92,796			2005	223,000
1975	85,258	1990	208,680	2006	230,000
1976	92,021	1991	189,435	2007	154,000
1977	87,615	1992	146,427		

The 136th Open Championship

Complete Scores

HOLE			1	2	3	4	5	6	7	8	9	10	11	12	13	14	15	16	17	18	
PAR	POSITION		4	4	4	4	4	5	4	3	4	4	4	4	3	5	4	3	4	4	TOTAL
Padraig Harrington	T8	Round 1	4	5	4	4	4	5	4	3	3	4	4	4	2	4	4	3	4	4	69
Republic of Ireland	T13	Round 2	4	4	4	4	4	5	3	3	4	5	4	4	3	4	5	3	4	6	73
£750,000	T3	Round 3	3	4	4	4	3	4	4	3	4	4	4	5	2	5	4	3	4	4	68
		Round 4	4	4	3	4	4	4	4	3	3	4	3	4	3	3	4	3	4	6	67 **-277**
	1	Playoff	3															3	4	5	15
Sergio Garcia	1	Round 1	3	4	4	4	4	4	4	3	4	3	4	3	2	4	4	4	3	4	65
Spain	1	Round 2	4	4	4	5	4	4	4	3	4	4	5	4	3	4	4	3	4	4	71
£450,000	1	Round 3	3	4	4	4	4	5	4	2	4	4	3	4	3	5	4	3	4	4	68
		Round 4	4	4	3	4	5	5	5	4	4	4	4	4	2	4	5	3	4	5	73 **-277**
	2	Playoff	5															3	4	4	16
Andres Romero	T25	Round 1	4	4	4	4	4	5	4	3	4	4	4	4	3	5	4	3	5	3	71
Argentina	T7	Round 2	3	5	3	3	4	4	4	3	6	4	4	5	3	3	4	3	5	4	70
£290,000	T10	Round 3	4	4	4	4	4	5	3	3	5	4	4	4	2	5	5	2	4	4	70
	3	Round 4	4	4	3	3	4	4	4	2	5	3	3	6	2	4	3	2	6	5	67 **-278**
Richard Green	T39	Round 1	3	4	4	4	5	4	4	3	3	4	4	5	3	4	6	4	4	4	72
Australia	T42	Round 2	4	5	4	4	5	4	4	3	4	5	4	4	3	5	3	3	4	5	73
£200,000	T31	Round 3	4	3	4	4	4	5	4	3	4	5	3	4	3	4	5	3	4	4	70
	T4	Round 4	4	3	3	4	4	4	4	3	3	4	4	4	2	3	4	3	3	5	64 **-279**
Ernie Els	T39	Round 1	3	4	5	4	4	4	4	3	4	5	4	4	3	4	4	3	5	5	72
South Africa	T13	Round 2	4	4	4	4	3	5	4	3	4	4	3	4	4	5	4	3	4	4	70
£200,000	T3	Round 3	4	3	4	4	4	8	4	2	4	4	3	3	2	5	4	2	4	4	68
	T4	Round 4	4	3	3	4	4	4	4	3	4	4	4	4	4	4	5	3	4	4	69 **-279**
Hunter Mahan	T60	Round 1	3	4	5	4	5	5	3	3	4	4	4	5	4	3	5	4	4	4	73
USA	T53	Round 2	4	3	5	4	4	5	4	4	4	3	3	5	3	5	4	3	4	6	73
£145,500	T31	Round 3	3	3	4	4	3	4	4	4	4	4	4	5	3	4	4	4	4	4	69
	T6	Round 4	4	4	3	4	4	4	4	3	4	3	4	4	3	4	4	3	3	4	65 **-280**
Stewart Cink	T8	Round 1	4	4	5	4	4	4	4	2	3	5	3	4	2	5	4	4	4	4	69
USA	T13	Round 2	3	4	5	3	4	5	4	3	4	4	4	6	3	5	4	4	4	4	73
£145,500	T3	Round 3	3	4	4	4	4	4	4	3	4	4	4	5	3	4	4	3	3	4	68
	T6	Round 4	4	4	4	3	4	5	4	3	5	4	3	4	3	4	5	2	4	5	70 **-280**

* Denotes amateurs

	HOLE		1	2	3	4	5	6	7	8	9	10	11	12	13	14	15	16	17	18	
	PAR	POSITION	4	4	4	4	4	5	4	3	4	4	4	4	3	5	4	3	4	4	TOTAL
Ben Curtis	T39	Round 1	4	4	4	4	4	5	3	4	5	4	3	5	4	4	4	3	4	4	72
USA	T53	Round 2	4	4	4	4	4	5	4	3	5	4	4	4	3	4	4	4	4	6	74
£94,750	T37	Round 3	4	4	3	4	3	5	4	3	4	4	4	5	3	4	4	3	4	5	70
	T8	Round 4	4	4	3	4	3	5	4	2	4	3	4	5	2	3	4	3	4	4	65 **-281**
Mike Weir	T25	Round 1	3	4	5	4	5	5	4	3	5	3	4	4	3	4	4	3	4	4	71
Canada	T3	Round 2	3	5	4	5	4	4	4	3	4	3	4	4	3	4	4	2	4	4	68
£94,750	T7	Round 3	4	3	5	4	4	5	3	4	4	4	4	4	3	4	5	3	4	5	72
	T8	Round 4	5	4	5	3	3	5	4	3	4	4	4	5	2	4	4	3	4	4	70 **-281**
K J Choi	T8	Round 1	3	4	3	3	4	4	5	3	4	4	4	4	2	5	5	3	4	5	69
South Korea	2	Round 2	3	4	5	4	4	4	4	4	4	4	3	4	3	4	3	3	4	5	69
£94,750	T3	Round 3	4	3	4	4	4	6	4	4	4	4	3	4	3	5	4	3	4	5	72
	T8	Round 4	4	4	4	3	4	5	4	3	6	4	4	5	2	4	4	3	4	4	71 **-281**
Steve Stricker	T25	Round 1	4	5	4	3	6	4	3	3	4	4	4	5	2	4	4	3	4	5	71
USA	T20	Round 2	4	4	4	4	3	4	3	3	4	6	3	4	3	5	4	4	5	5	72
£94,750	2	Round 3	3	3	3	4	3	5	3	3	4	4	4	4	2	4	4	3	4	4	64
	T8	Round 4	4	4	4	3	5	5	4	3	5	4	4	4	3	5	4	4	5	4	74 **-281**
Markus Brier	T3	Round 1	3	5	3	3	6	5	4	3	3	4	3	4	2	5	4	3	4	4	68
Austria	T20	Round 2	4	4	4	4	5	4	4	3	4	5	4	4	4	4	6	3	4	5	75
£58,571	T20	Round 3	3	4	5	3	4	5	4	3	4	4	4	4	3	5	4	3	4	4	70
	T12	Round 4	4	4	4	4	4	5	4	3	4	3	3	4	3	4	4	4	4	4	69 **-282**
Tiger Woods	T8	Round 1	4	4	3	4	3	4	4	4	3	4	4	5	4	5	4	2	4	4	69
USA	T20	Round 2	6	3	4	4	5	5	4	4	4	4	4	4	3	4	4	3	4	5	74
£58,571	T15	Round 3	4	5	4	3	3	5	3	3	4	5	4	4	3	4	4	3	4	4	69
	T12	Round 4	4	4	4	3	3	5	4	4	4	4	5	4	2	4	5	3	4	4	70 **-282**
Justin Rose	T104	Round 1	3	4	6	3	4	4	4	3	3	5	4	5	3	5	5	3	5	6	75
England	T42	Round 2	3	4	4	4	5	4	4	2	4	4	4	4	4	4	4	3	5	4	70
£58,571	T15	Round 3	4	4	4	3	3	4	5	4	3	4	4	4	3	4	3	3	4	4	67
	T12	Round 4	5	3	4	4	3	5	4	3	4	4	4	4	3	5	4	3	4	4	70 **-282**
Pelle Edberg	T39	Round 1	4	5	3	4	4	6	4	3	4	4	4	4	4	4	4	3	4	4	72
Sweden	T42	Round 2	4	4	3	3	4	6	3	3	3	4	4	4	3	4	6	4	6	5	73
£58,571	T15	Round 3	4	4	4	4	4	4	4	3	4	3	4	4	3	4	4	3	4	3	67
	T12	Round 4	3	5	4	4	4	5	4	3	5	3	4	4	3	4	4	3	5	3	70 **-282**
Miguel Angel Jimenez	T8	Round 1	4	4	4	3	4	4	4	3	4	5	4	4	3	4	4	3	4	4	69
	T3	Round 2	4	4	4	3	4	5	4	3	5	5	4	4	3	4	4	2	4	4	70
Spain	T10	Round 3	4	3	4	4	4	5	4	3	4	5	3	4	3	7	3	3	5	4	72
£58,571	**T12**	Round 4	4	5	4	4	4	5	4	3	4	4	4	4	3	4	5	3	4	3	71 **-282**
Jim Furyk	T13	Round 1	4	3	4	4	5	5	3	3	3	5	4	4	2	5	4	3	4	5	70
USA	T5	Round 2	3	5	3	4	4	4	3	3	4	5	3	5	3	5	4	3	4	5	70
£58,571	T10	Round 3	4	4	4	4	4	5	4	3	5	3	4	4	4	4	3	4	3	5	71
	T12	Round 4	5	3	4	4	5	5	4	3	3	4	5	5	3	4	4	3	4	3	71 **-282**
Paul Broadhurst	T25	Round 1	4	4	4	3	3	6	5	3	4	4	3	5	3	4	4	3	4	5	71
England	T13	Round 2	4	4	3	4	4	4	4	2	4	5	5	5	3	4	4	3	4	5	71
£58,571	T3	Round 3	3	4	3	4	4	7	4	3	5	4	4	3	3	4	3	3	3	4	68
	T12	Round 4	4	3	4	4	3	5	4	3	5	4	5	5	3	4	4	4	4	4	72 **-282**
Paul McGinley	2	Round 1	3	3	4	3	4	5	3	3	4	4	4	4	2	4	5	4	4	4	67
Republic of Ireland	T13	Round 2	5	4	6	3	4	6	4	3	4	5	3	4	3	6	4	3	4	4	75
£46,000	T3	Round 3	4	3	4	3	4	5	4	3	3	4	4	4	3	4	4	4	4	4	68
	19	Round 4	4	5	3	5	4	5	6	3	4	5	3	4	3	3	4	3	4	5	73 **-283**

HOLE			1	2	3	4	5	6	7	8	9	10	11	12	13	14	15	16	17	18	
PAR	POSITION		4	4	4	4	4	5	4	3	4	4	4	4	3	5	4	3	4	4	TOTAL
Pat Perez	T60	Round 1	5	4	4	4	3	4	4	3	5	4	4	4	2	5	5	3	4	6	73
USA	T20	Round 2	4	3	4	4	4	4	5	2	4	4	4	6	3	4	3	3	4	5	70
£42,000	T24	Round 3	4	5	3	4	4	4	4	3	4	4	3	4	3	5	4	4	5	4	71
	T20	Round 4	4	4	4	4	4	5	4	3	4	3	5	4	3	4	4	3	4	4	70 **-284**
Zach Johnson	T60	Round 1	4	4	4	4	6	4	4	3	4	3	5	4	3	4	5	4	4	4	73
USA	T53	Round 2	4	4	4	3	4	5	5	6	4	3	4	4	3	4	4	3	4	5	73
£42,000	T24	Round 3	3	4	4	4	4	5	4	3	4	4	4	4	2	4	4	3	4	4	68
	T20	Round 4	4	3	4	4	4	4	5	3	4	4	4	4	2	5	4	3	4	5	70 **-284**
Rich Beem	T13	Round 1	4	5	3	4	3	4	3	4	4	4	4	4	3	4	5	3	5	4	70
USA	T20	Round 2	3	4	4	4	4	4	4	3	4	6	3	4	4	5	4	3	4	6	73
£42,000	T15	Round 3	4	4	3	4	5	4	5	3	4	5	3	4	2	4	4	4	3	4	69
	T20	Round 4	6	4	4	3	4	5	4	2	3	4	4	5	2	5	5	3	5	4	72 **-284**
Mark Calcavecchia	T78	Round 1	4	4	4	4	4	6	4	3	3	5	4	4	3	5	5	3	4	5	74
USA	T31	Round 2	4	4	4	4	4	4	4	3	4	4	4	4	3	5	4	3	4	4	70
£35,563	T37	Round 3	5	5	4	4	4	4	5	4	4	4	3	4	3	4	4	2	5	4	72
	T23	Round 4	6	4	3	4	4	4	4	3	4	3	5	4	3	4	4	3	4	3	69 **-285**
Jonathan Byrd	T60	Round 1	4	4	4	3	4	7	4	2	4	6	5	4	3	4	3	4	4	4	73
USA	T42	Round 2	3	5	4	4	3	6	4	3	3	4	4	4	3	5	5	4	4	4	72
£35,563	T31	Round 3	4	4	4	3	4	5	4	4	5	4	4	4	2	4	4	3	4	4	70
	T23	Round 4	4	4	3	4	5	4	4	3	5	4	4	5	2	4	4	3	4	4	70 **-285**
Retief Goosen	T13	Round 1	4	5	4	3	4	4	3	3	4	4	4	3	2	5	6	4	4	4	70
South Africa	T7	Round 2	4	3	4	5	5	4	3	3	4	3	4	4	4	5	5	3	3	5	71
£35,563	T24	Round 3	4	4	4	3	4	4	4	4	5	4	4	3	2	4	4	6	5	5	73
	T23	Round 4	4	4	4	4	4	5	4	2	4	3	4	4	4	4	5	3	5	4	71 **-285**
Chris DiMarco	T78	Round 1	4	5	5	4	4	3	3	2	4	5	4	5	4	5	4	3	5	5	74
USA	T31	Round 2	4	3	4	4	4	5	4	3	4	5	3	4	3	4	3	4	4	5	70
£35,563	T3	Round 3	3	4	4	3	4	4	5	2	4	4	3	4	3	4	4	4	3	4	66
	T23	Round 4	4	3	5	4	3	4	4	5	5	4	4	4	3	4	5	3	5	6	75 **-285**
Ian Poulter	T60	Round 1	3	5	4	4	4	4	4	3	5	4	3	5	4	5	4	3	4	5	73
England	T53	Round 2	4	4	5	4	3	4	5	4	4	4	3	5	3	4	5	4	4	4	73
£28,179	T37	Round 3	3	4	4	4	3	4	4	3	4	4	3	4	3	4	6	4	5	4	70
	T27	Round 4	4	5	4	4	5	6	3	2	4	4	4	4	3	5	3	2	4	4	70 **-286**
Adam Scott	T60	Round 1	4	5	4	4	5	5	4	3	4	5	5	4	3	4	4	3	3	4	73
Australia	T20	Round 2	4	4	4	3	4	4	4	3	4	5	4	4	3	5	4	3	4	4	70
£28,179	T31	Round 3	4	4	4	4	4	4	4	2	5	4	4	5	3	6	4	3	4	4	72
	T27	Round 4	4	4	4	4	5	4	4	3	4	4	4	4	3	4	4	4	4	4	71 **-286**
Rod Pampling	T13	Round 1	4	4	3	4	4	4	4	3	4	4	4	5	2	5	4	3	4	5	70
Australia	T13	Round 2	4	3	3	4	6	4	4	3	4	4	4	4	4	4	4	3	5	5	72
£28,179	T24	Round 3	4	4	5	3	4	5	4	3	6	4	4	4	3	3	4	4	4	4	72
	T27	Round 4	5	5	4	4	4	5	4	3	4	4	4	4	3	4	3	4	4	4	72 **-286**
Paul Casey	T39	Round 1	4	4	5	3	4	5	4	3	4	4	4	4	3	6	4	4	3	4	72
England	T42	Round 2	3	4	5	4	4	6	4	3	4	4	4	5	3	4	4	3	4	5	73
£28,179	T24	Round 3	4	4	4	4	5	4	3	3	4	4	4	4	2	4	4	3	4	5	69
	T27	Round 4	3	4	4	4	4	5	4	4	4	5	3	5	3	5	4	3	4	4	72 **-286**
Lucas Glover	T25	Round 1	3	3	4	4	5	4	3	3	4	4	4	6	3	5	4	4	4	4	71
USA	T20	Round 2	4	4	4	4	4	4	5	4	4	3	4	5	3	5	4	3	4	4	72
£28,179	T20	Round 3	4	5	4	4	4	4	3	3	4	4	4	6	2	4	4	3	4	4	70
	T27	Round 4	4	5	4	4	5	7	3	3	4	3	6	4	3	3	4	3	4	4	73 **-286**

HOLE			1	2	3	4	5	6	7	8	9	10	11	12	13	14	15	16	17	18	
PAR	POSITION		4	4	4	4	5	4	4	3	4	4	4	5	3	5	4	3	4	4	TOTAL
J J Henry	T13	Round 1	4	4	4	4	5	4	4	2	4	4	4	5	3	4	3	3	4	5	70
USA	T7	Round 2	4	5	4	4	4	4	4	4	4	4	4	3	4	4	4	3	4	4	71
£28,179	T15	Round 3	3	4	4	4	3	7	4	3	4	4	4	4	3	5	5	2	4	4	71
	T27	Round 4	5	5	3	4	4	5	4	2	4	4	4	4	3	5	4	3	5	6	74 -**286**
Vijay Singh	T39	Round 1	4	3	4	4	5	4	4	3	4	4	4	5	3	3	4	4	4	6	72
Fiji	T20	Round 2	4	4	4	4	3	4	3	3	4	4	4	4	4	4	5	3	4	6	71
£28,179	T10	Round 3	4	4	3	4	4	4	4	3	4	4	4	4	3	4	4	3	4	4	68
	T27	Round 4	4	6	3	4	4	4	4	4	5	4	4	5	3	4	5	3	4	5	75 -**286**
Angel Cabrera	T3	Round 1	4	4	4	3	4	5	3	3	4	4	4	5	3	4	3	3	4	4	68
Argentina	T7	Round 2	4	4	5	4	5	5	4	3	4	4	4	4	3	5	4	4	4	3	73
£24,000	T20	Round 3	4	4	4	4	4	4	4	3	5	5	4	4	3	4	4	4	4	4	72
	34	Round 4	4	5	3	4	4	6	6	4	4	5	3	4	2	4	4	4	4	4	74 -**287**
Mark Foster	T118	Round 1	4	4	5	4	6	4	4	4	6	4	4	4	2	6	3	3	4	5	76
England	T53	Round 2	4	4	4	3	4	4	4	2	3	5	4	4	4	5	5	3	4	4	70
£20,107	T53	Round 3	4	4	5	4	4	5	4	3	4	4	5	3	3	5	4	3	4	5	73
	T35	Round 4	3	4	3	5	4	6	3	4	4	4	4	5	2	4	4	2	4	4	69 -**288**
Niclas Fasth	T104	Round 1	4	6	4	4	5	4	4	3	5	4	3	4	4	5	4	3	4	5	75
Sweden	T31	Round 2	4	3	4	3	3	4	4	3	5	3	4	6	3	5	4	3	4	4	69
£20,107	T45	Round 3	4	3	4	4	4	4	4	4	4	4	4	5	3	5	4	4	5	4	73
	T35	Round 4	4	5	4	4	3	5	4	3	4	5	4	3	2	4	4	4	4	5	71 -**288**
Charley Hoffman	T104	Round 1	4	5	4	4	3	4	4	3	5	5	4	4	3	5	4	5	5	4	75
USA	T31	Round 2	4	4	4	4	4	4	3	3	4	3	3	3	4	4	4	3	5	6	69
£20,107	T37	Round 3	4	4	4	3	4	5	5	2	5	4	5	3	2	4	5	4	5	5	72
	T35	Round 4	4	3	4	3	3	6	4	3	4	4	4	5	5	4	4	4	4	4	72 -**288**
Shaun Micheel	T13	Round 1	4	4	4	3	4	4	4	3	5	4	4	4	3	5	4	3	4	4	70
USA	T53	Round 2	4	4	4	4	5	4	5	2	4	4	4	4	3	7	5	3	5	5	76
£20,107	T37	Round 3	3	5	4	4	4	5	4	4	3	5	4	4	3	3	3	3	4	5	70
	T35	Round 4	4	4	4	4	3	5	4	4	5	4	5	4	3	4	4	3	4	4	72 -**288**
Boo Weekley	T3	Round 1	3	4	6	4	4	4	4	2	4	4	4	4	3	4	3	3	4	4	68
USA	T5	Round 2	4	5	4	4	4	4	4	3	4	3	4	4	3	5	5	4	4	4	72
£20,107	T31	Round 3	4	4	3	4	4	6	4	5	4	4	4	4	3	4	4	4	5	5	75
	T35	Round 4	4	4	6	4	6	5	4	3	4	4	4	4	2	4	4	3	4	4	73 -**288**
Lee Westwood	T25	Round 1	3	4	5	4	4	5	4	3	4	5	4	4	3	5	2	4	4	4	71
England	T7	Round 2	4	4	5	4	4	4	4	2	5	4	4	4	3	3	4	3	4	5	70
£20,107	T24	Round 3	3	3	5	4	4	5	4	3	4	4	4	6	3	4	4	4	4	5	73
	T35	Round 4	4	3	4	4	5	5	4	3	5	4	4	4	3	4	6	4	4	4	74 -**288**
Nick Watney	T39	Round 1	4	5	4	4	5	5	4	2	4	4	5	4	2	4	5	3	4	4	72
USA	T20	Round 2	4	3	5	4	4	6	4	2	4	4	3	5	3	4	5	3	4	4	71
£20,107	T20	Round 3	3	4	4	4	4	4	4	3	5	4	4	4	2	5	5	3	4	4	70
	T35	Round 4	4	6	4	4	4	5	4	3	5	4	4	4	3	5	4	3	5	4	75 -**288**
Ryan Moore	T39	Round 1	4	4	4	4	5	4	4	3	5	4	3	3	3	4	5	3	5	5	72
USA	T31	Round 2	4	4	5	4	4	6	4	3	4	6	4	4	3	4	3	3	4	3	72
£16,375	T50	Round 3	4	3	4	4	5	5	6	2	4	4	4	4	3	4	5	4	5	4	74
	T42	Round 4	6	3	4	4	4	5	4	3	4	4	3	4	3	4	5	3	4	4	71 -**289**
Rory McIlroy*	T3	Round 1	4	4	4	4	3	5	4	3	4	3	4	4	2	5	4	3	4	4	68
Northern Ireland	T31	Round 2	4	5	4	3	5	5	4	3	6	4	5	5	3	4	4	3	5	4	76
	T45	Round 3	4	4	4	5	4	6	4	3	5	4	5	3	3	4	4	3	4	4	73
	T42	Round 4	4	4	4	4	5	6	4	3	4	4	4	4	2	4	5	4	4	3	72 -**289**

HOLE			1	2	3	4	5	6	7	8	9	10	11	12	13	14	15	16	17	18	
PAR	POSITION		4	4	4	4	4	5	4	3	4	4	4	4	3	5	4	3	4	4	TOTAL
Nick Dougherty	T25	Round 1	3	4	6	3	5	4	4	2	4	4	4	5	3	5	4	4	3	4	71
England	T42	Round 2	6	4	4	3	4	5	4	3	3	4	4	4	4	5	5	3	5	4	74
£16,375	T24	Round 3	4	3	3	4	4	5	4	3	4	4	4	4	3	5	4	4	3	4	69
	T42	Round 4	4	4	5	4	6	7	4	2	3	4	4	3	3	5	4	4	4	5	75 **-289**
Carl Pettersson	T13	Round 1	5	3	5	4	4	4	4	3	4	5	4	4	2	4	4	3	4	4	70
Sweden	T42	Round 2	5	3	6	4	4	5	4	3	4	5	4	4	2	5	4	3	4	6	75
£14,500	T50	Round 3	3	5	5	4	4	5	4	4	4	5	4	4	2	4	4	4	4	4	73
	T45	Round 4	4	5	4	4	4	6	4	2	4	4	4	5	3	4	4	3	4	4	72 **-290**
John Senden	T39	Round 1	4	4	6	3	4	4	4	3	4	5	3	5	3	4	5	3	4	4	72
Australia	T53	Round 2	4	4	4	3	5	5	4	4	4	4	5	4	4	4	4	3	4	5	74
£14,500	T45	Round 3	4	4	5	4	4	4	3	3	4	4	4	5	3	3	4	3	4	6	71
	T45	Round 4	4	5	4	3	4	5	4	3	5	4	4	5	3	4	5	3	4	4	73 **-290**
Arron Oberholser	T60	Round 1	4	4	5	5	4	5	4	3	4	4	4	4	2	5	5	2	4	5	73
USA	T31	Round 2	4	3	4	3	4	5	4	3	4	4	4	4	3	5	5	3	4	5	71
£14,500	T37	Round 3	5	3	5	4	4	5	3	4	4	4	4	4	2	4	4	3	5	5	72
	T45	Round 4	4	5	4	5	4	5	3	4	4	5	5	4	2	4	4	4	4	4	74 **-290**
Ross Bain	T60	Round 1	5	3	4	5	4	6	3	3	4	5	4	4	2	5	5	3	4	4	73
Scotland	T31	Round 2	4	4	5	4	5	6	4	3	4	3	3	5	2	4	5	3	4	3	71
£14,500	T37	Round 3	4	4	4	3	4	4	5	4	4	4	4	4	4	4	4	4	4	4	72
	T45	Round 4	4	4	3	4	4	5	6	4	4	4	4	5	3	4	4	3	4	5	74 **-290**
Won Joon Lee	T60	Round 1	4	4	5	3	4	6	4	3	4	5	4	4	3	4	4	3	4	5	73
Australia	T53	Round 2	3	4	4	4	5	7	4	3	5	4	3	4	3	5	3	4	3	5	73
£13,000	T37	Round 3	5	6	4	4	4	4	4	3	4	4	4	3	2	5	4	3	3	4	70
	T49	Round 4	5	4	4	3	4	5	5	3	6	4	5	4	3	4	4	4	5	3	75 **-291**
Jerry Kelly	T78	Round 1	3	4	5	4	5	6	4	3	3	5	4	5	3	4	4	3	4	5	74
USA	T31	Round 2	4	4	4	4	3	5	5	3	4	4	4	4	3	4	4	3	4	4	70
£13,000	T31	Round 3	3	4	4	4	5	5	5	4	4	3	4	4	3	5	3	3	4	4	71
	T49	Round 4	4	6	3	7	4	4	4	3	4	4	5	4	3	4	4	3	4	6	76 **-291**
Kevin Stadler	T104	Round 1	4	4	6	4	4	5	4	3	4	3	3	6	3	4	4	4	4	6	75
USA	T53	Round 2	4	4	4	3	3	6	6	3	4	3	4	4	4	4	4	3	4	4	71
£12,125	T62	Round 3	4	3	4	4	4	4	4	2	4	6	4	4	4	4	7	3	4	5	74
	T51	Round 4	4	4	4	3	4	7	4	3	5	4	4	5	2	4	4	3	5	4	73 **-293**
Tom Lehman	T60	Round 1	4	5	5	4	5	5	4	3	5	4	3	4	2	4	4	3	5	4	73
USA	T53	Round 2	4	4	4	3	4	5	4	3	4	4	4	4	3	6	4	4	4	5	73
£12,125	T62	Round 3	4	3	4	4	5	7	4	3	3	4	4	4	4	4	6	3	4	4	74
	T51	Round 4	5	4	5	4	4	5	3	3	4	4	4	4	3	4	4	4	4	5	73 **-293**
Gregory Bourdy	T13	Round 1	4	4	4	3	5	5	3	2	5	4	4	4	3	5	4	3	4	4	70
France	T13	Round 2	3	5	4	4	4	5	4	3	4	5	3	4	3	5	4	3	5	4	72
£11,375	T53	Round 3	4	3	4	3	4	8	5	3	7	4	4	4	2	4	4	3	5	6	77
	T53	Round 4	4	4	4	4	6	5	4	4	4	4	4	4	3	4	4	3	3	7	75 **-294**
Thomas Bjorn	T13	Round 1	5	3	4	4	5	4	3	3	5	4	3	5	2	5	4	3	4	4	70
Denmark	T42	Round 2	4	4	4	4	4	5	5	3	4	4	4	4	4	5	4	4	4	5	75
£11,375	T53	Round 3	4	4	4	4	4	5	4	4	4	4	4	4	3	5	4	4	5	4	74
	T53	Round 4	4	4	4	5	3	6	4	3	4	5	4	4	2	5	5	4	4	5	75 **-294**
David Howell	T39	Round 1	5	5	6	3	4	4	3	2	5	4	4	5	2	4	4	4	4	4	72
England	T53	Round 2	4	4	5	4	4	4	4	2	4	5	5	5	3	4	4	3	5	5	74
£11,375	T53	Round 3	4	4	4	4	5	5	4	3	5	3	4	5	3	4	4	4	4	4	73
	T53	Round 4	4	4	4	5	4	5	5	4	5	5	5	4	2	4	4	3	5	3	75 **-294**

HOLE			1	2	3	4	5	6	7	8	9	10	11	12	13	14	15	16	17	18	
PAR	POSITION		4	4	4	4	5	4	3	4	4	4	4	3	5	4	3	4	4	4	TOTAL
Brian Davis	T78	Round 1	4	5	3	5	6	4	4	3	3	5	3	4	3	5	4	4	5	4	74
England	T53	Round 2	4	4	4	4	4	4	4	3	3	4	4	4	3	5	5	4	4	5	72
£11,375	T45	Round 3	4	4	3	4	4	4	4	4	4	4	3	5	3	4	4	3	4	6	71
	T53	Round 4	5	4	4	4	4	6	4	4	6	4	4	6	3	3	4	4	4	4	77 **-294**
Anders Hansen	T39	Round 1	4	4	4	3	5	5	4	3	4	4	4	5	2	4	4	4	4	5	72
Denmark	T42	Round 2	4	4	3	3	4	4	4	4	5	5	4	5	3	4	4	4	4	5	73
£10,800	T53	Round 3	4	4	4	4	4	4	4	3	5	3	4	5	3	5	4	4	5	5	74
	T57	Round 4	4	4	3	5	5	5	5	3	4	4	4	4	3	6	5	3	4	5	76 **-295**
Michael Campbell	T3	Round 1	4	3	4	3	4	4	4	3	4	5	4	5	2	4	4	4	3	4	68
New Zealand	T53	Round 2	4	5	5	4	4	5	4	3	5	6	4	5	2	4	6	3	4	5	78
£10,800	T50	Round 3	4	4	5	4	4	4	4	3	4	5	4	4	3	5	4	3	3	5	72
	T57	Round 4	5	5	5	5	4	5	3	3	5	5	4	4	3	5	4	3	4	5	77 **-295**
Scott Verplank	T39	Round 1	4	4	4	3	4	4	3	3	6	4	4	4	3	5	5	3	4	5	72
USA	T42	Round 2	4	4	3	5	4	4	4	4	4	4	4	3	3	6	5	3	4	5	73
£10,800	T45	Round 3	4	3	4	4	4	4	5	3	3	4	5	4	3	5	5	3	4	5	72
	T57	Round 4	4	4	4	5	5	6	4	5	5	5	4	3	3	5	4	4	4	4	78 **-295**
Trevor Immelman	T25	Round 1	4	4	4	3	4	5	4	3	3	4	5	4	4	4	4	3	4	5	71
South Africa	T42	Round 2	4	4	4	4	5	4	4	3	4	5	4	4	3	4	5	4	4	5	74
£10,500	T67	Round 3	4	4	3	5	6	4	4	4	5	4	5	4	3	5	4	4	4	5	77
	T60	Round 4	4	3	4	4	4	5	5	3	5	4	4	4	3	5	5	4	4	4	74 **-296**
Mark O'Meara	T78	Round 1	4	4	5	4	4	5	3	3	4	4	4	4	3	5	4	4	5	5	74
USA	T53	Round 2	3	3	4	4	4	4	5	3	4	5	3	5	3	6	4	3	5	4	72
£10,500	T67	Round 3	4	4	5	4	4	6	5	3	5	4	5	4	3	5	5	3	4	3	76
	T60	Round 4	3	4	5	4	4	5	5	2	6	4	5	4	3	5	4	3	4	4	74 **-296**
Toru Taniguchi	T39	Round 1	3	4	3	4	5	4	4	3	4	4	3	5	3	5	4	5	4	5	72
Japan	T31	Round 2	4	4	4	4	6	4	5	3	4	3	3	4	4	4	5	2	4	5	72
£10,500	T62	Round 3	4	3	4	4	5	6	4	3	4	4	3	5	4	5	5	4	3	6	76
	T60	Round 4	4	4	4	4	4	5	5	3	4	4	5	5	3	6	4	3	5	4	76 **-296**
Jon Bevan	T60	Round 1	4	4	4	5	5	5	3	3	4	4	4	3	2	5	5	4	4	5	73
England	T53	Round 2	4	3	5	5	4	3	4	4	4	5	4	3	3	5	5	3	4	5	73
£10,250	70	Round 3	5	3	4	4	5	6	4	3	5	5	4	5	3	4	5	4	5	5	79
	T63	Round 4	4	4	3	5	4	5	4	3	4	4	5	6	2	3	5	3	4	4	72 **-297**
Luke Donald	T13	Round 1	4	4	3	3	4	5	4	3	4	4	4	5	2	4	4	4	4	5	70
England	T53	Round 2	4	3	6	4	4	8	4	3	4	5	3	3	3	4	6	4	4	4	76
£10,250	T53	Round 3	3	4	4	3	4	6	3	2	5	4	5	4	3	4	5	4	5	5	73
	T63	Round 4	5	4	5	5	4	6	5	3	4	4	4	4	3	5	5	3	5	4	78 **-297**
Raphael Jacquelin	T78	Round 1	4	5	4	4	4	4	4	2	4	4	4	4	2	5	4	4	4	8	74
France	T20	Round 2	4	4	5	3	4	4	4	2	4	5	4	5	3	4	4	2	4	4	69
£10,050	T53	Round 3	4	4	5	4	4	5	4	4	5	5	4	5	3	4	5	3	4	4	76
	T65	Round 4	4	4	4	4	6	4	4	5	3	4	4	5	3	5	5	4	5	6	79 **-298**
Sandy Lyle	T60	Round 1	4	4	5	4	5	4	4	3	5	4	4	4	3	5	3	3	4	5	73
Scotland	T53	Round 2	4	3	5	4	5	4	4	3	4	5	3	4	3	4	5	3	5	5	63
£10,050	T53	Round 3	3	4	4	4	4	5	5	3	4	5	4	5	3	3	4	4	4	5	73
	T65	Round 4	4	6	4	4	4	8	4	4	4	4	5	4	2	4	4	3	5	6	79 **-298**
Sean O'Hair	T25	Round 1	3	5	4	5	4	4	4	3	5	3	4	4	3	5	4	3	4	4	71
USA	T53	Round 2	5	4	5	4	4	6	4	2	4	4	4	4	3	4	5	3	4	6	75
£9,850	T62	Round 3	3	4	5	4	4	5	5	3	4	4	4	6	3	4	4	4	4	4	74
	T67	Round 4	4	4	5	4	4	6	5	4	6	4	4	5	3	5	4	3	4	5	79 **-299**

	POSITION	1	2	3	4	5	6	7	8	9	10	11	12	13	14	15	16	17	18	TOTAL
HOLE / PAR		4	4	4	4	4	5	4	3	4	4	4	4	3	5	4	3	4	4	
Alastair Forsyth	T13	5	4	5	4	4	4	4	3	4	4	4	4	2	4	4	3	4	4	Round 1 — 70
Scotland	T7	4	3	5	4	4	4	4	4	4	4	5	4	2	5	4	3	4	4	Round 2 — 71
£9,850	T53	4	4	5	5	5	6	4	4	4	5	4	4	3	5	5	4	4	3	Round 3 — 78
	T67	4	5	4	5	4	7	5	4	4	4	5	4	3	6	4	3	4	5	Round 4 — 80 **-299**
Fredrik	T39	3	4	4	4	4	3	4	3	5	4	5	5	3	6	4	3	3	5	Round 1 — 72
Andersson Hed	T20	4	4	4	4	3	4	4	2	5	5	3	4	4	4	5	3	4	5	Round 2 — 71
Sweden	T67	5	5	4	4	5	5	4	2	5	4	4	4	4	7	4	3	5	5	Round 3 — 79
£9,650	**T69**	5	4	5	4	3	5	4	3	5	4	4	5	3	5	6	3	5	5	Round 4 — 78 **-300**
Peter Hanson	T13	4	4	4	3	4	4	4	4	4	4	4	4	2	4	4	3	5	5	Round 1 — 70
Sweden	T31	5	4	4	3	5	5	4	5	4	4	3	4	3	5	5	3	4	4	Round 2 — 74
£9,650	T62	4	4	4	3	4	7	5	3	5	4	5	5	2	4	5	3	5	4	Round 3 — 76
	T69	4	5	4	4	5	6	5	3	6	4	4	4	3	6	4	3	5	5	Round 4 — 80 **-300**

NON QUALIFIERS AFTER 36 HOLES

(Leading 10 professionals and ties receive £3,200 each, next 20 professionals and ties receive £2,650 each, next 20 professionals and ties receive £2,375 each, remainder of professionals receive £2,100 each.)

	POSITION	1	2	3	4	5	6	7	8	9	10	11	12	13	14	15	16	17	18	TOTAL
HOLE / PAR		4	4	4	4	4	5	4	3	4	4	4	4	3	5	4	3	4	4	
Matthew Zions	T39	3	4	5	4	5	4	5	3	3	4	4	4	3	4	4	4	4	5	Round 1 — 72
Australia	**T71**	4	3	4	5	4	4	4	3	4	4	4	4	3	4	5	5	5	6	Round 2 — 75 **-147**
Henrik Stenson	T25	3	4	4	4	4	5	3	3	4	4	4	5	3	4	4	4	4	5	Round 1 — 71
Sweden	**T71**	4	5	4	3	4	5	5	6	4	4	4	4	3	4	5	3	4	5	Round 2 — 76 **-147**
Tom Pernice Jnr	T78	4	4	4	4	4	5	5	3	4	5	4	3	3	4	4	4	5	5	Round 1 — 74
USA	**T71**	4	5	4	4	4	5	4	3	4	4	4	4	4	5	5	3	3	4	Round 2 — 73 **-147**
Johan Edfors	T39	4	5	3	4	4	5	5	2	4	4	4	4	4	4	5	3	4	4	Round 1 — 72
Sweden	**T71**	4	5	4	4	4	5	4	3	5	6	4	4	3	4	5	3	4	4	Round 2 — 75 **-147**
Joe Durant	T128	4	4	4	4	6	6	4	3	5	5	4	4	2	5	5	3	4	5	Round 1 — 77
USA	**T71**	4	4	4	4	4	5	4	3	4	5	3	4	3	5	4	2	4	4	Round 2 — 70 **-147**
Peter Fowler	T78	4	5	6	4	4	5	4	3	4	4	4	4	2	5	4	4	3	5	Round 1 — 74
Australia	**T71**	4	5	4	3	4	4	3	3	4	4	4	5	3	5	4	4	5	5	Round 2 — 73 **-147**
Justin Leonard	T78	3	4	4	4	4	4	4	4	4	5	3	5	3	5	5	3	5	5	Round 1 — 74
USA	**T71**	4	3	4	4	5	5	4	3	6	4	3	5	3	4	5	3	4	4	Round 2 — 73 **-147**
Paul Lawrie	T60	4	4	6	4	4	4	4	3	4	4	4	4	3	6	5	3	4	3	Round 1 — 73
Scotland	**T71**	4	3	5	4	5	5	4	3	4	4	5	3	3	5	4	3	4	6	Round 2 — 74 **-147**
Colin Montgomerie	T60	4	4	5	4	4	4	5	3	4	4	4	4	3	5	3	4	4	5	Round 1 — 73
Scotland	**T71**	3	4	4	4	5	6	4	3	5	4	4	5	4	4	4	3	4	4	Round 2 — 74 **-147**
Tomohiro Kondo	T78	3	3	5	4	5	6	4	4	5	3	5	4	3	3	5	3	4	5	Round 1 — 74
Japan	**T71**	4	4	4	4	4	4	4	4	4	4	3	4	4	6	4	3	4	5	Round 2 — 73 **-147**
David Toms	T25	4	5	3	4	4	5	3	3	4	4	4	4	3	4	5	3	4	5	Round 1 — 71
USA	**T81**	4	4	5	4	4	4	4	3	4	4	5	4	4	5	5	4	5	5	Round 2 — 77 **-148**
Phil Mickelson	T25	4	4	5	4	4	4	4	3	4	4	4	4	3	4	4	3	4	5	Round 1 — 71
USA	**T81**	4	5	4	4	5	4	5	3	4	4	4	5	3	5	5	3	4	6	Round 2 — 77 **-148**
Brett Quigley	T39	4	4	4	4	4	5	2	4	4	4	4	3	3	6	4	3	3	7	Round 1 — 72
USA	**T81**	4	5	4	4	5	6	4	2	4	4	4	4	4	5	5	4	4	4	Round 2 — 76 **-148**

HOLE			1	2	3	4	5	6	7	8	9	10	11	12	13	14	15	16	17	18	
PAR	POSITION		4	4	4	4	5	5	4	3	4	4	4	4	3	5	4	3	4	4	TOTAL
Terry Pilkadaris	T78	Round 1	4	4	4	4	5	5	4	3	4	5	4	4	2	5	5	4	4	4	74
Australia	**T81**	Round 2	4	4	3	4	6	6	3	3	4	5	4	4	4	4	5	3	4	4	74 -**148**
Benn Barham	T104	Round 1	4	5	4	4	5	5	4	3	4	4	4	5	2	5	5	3	5	4	75
England	**T81**	Round 2	4	4	6	3	3	5	4	3	4	6	4	4	3	4	4	3	4	5	73 -**148**
John Rollins	T39	Round 1	4	3	5	3	5	5	3	3	5	4	4	4	3	5	4	3	5	4	72
USA	**T81**	Round 2	5	4	5	4	5	5	5	3	5	5	3	4	3	5	4	3	4	4	76 -**148**
Darren Clarke	T39	Round 1	5	4	4	4	6	6	3	3	4	4	3	4	3	4	4	3	4	4	72
Northern Ireland	**T81**	Round 2	4	4	5	4	3	4	4	3	5	4	4	4	3	6	5	4	4	6	76 -**148**
Drew Weaver*	T118	Round 1	3	3	5	4	6	4	4	3	4	5	4	4	4	5	5	4	4	5	76
USA	**T81**	Round 2	3	4	3	4	4	4	5	4	4	4	4	4	3	6	5	3	4	4	72 -**148**
Toshi Izawa	T104	Round 1	4	6	5	4	4	5	4	4	3	3	4	5	4	4	4	4	4	4	75
Japan	**T81**	Round 2	4	4	4	4	4	4	4	4	4	4	4	5	3	4	5	3	4	5	73 -**148**
Gregory Havret	T39	Round 1	5	4	4	4	3	4	5	3	4	4	3	5	3	4	5	3	4	5	72
France	**T81**	Round 2	3	6	4	4	4	5	3	3	5	5	4	5	4	4	5	3	4	5	76 -**148**
Ross Fisher	T78	Round 1	4	4	4	4	4	4	4	3	4	4	4	6	3	4	5	5	4	4	74
England	**T91**	Round 2	3	4	4	4	5	5	3	3	4	4	4	6	4	5	5	3	4	5	75 -**149**
Brett Wetterich	T104	Round 1	4	5	5	3	4	6	4	3	5	4	4	5	3	3	4	4	4	5	75
USA	**T91**	Round 2	4	4	3	4	4	4	4	5	3	6	4	4	3	5	5	3	4	5	74 -**149**
David Frost	T78	Round 1	4	5	4	4	5	4	3	3	4	5	4	5	3	5	4	4	4	4	74
South Africa	**T91**	Round 2	4	4	5	3	5	5	4	3	4	4	4	4	3	5	5	4	4	5	75 -**149**
Charles Howell III	T60	Round 1	5	4	3	4	4	5	4	3	4	5	3	4	3	5	4	4	4	5	73
USA	**T91**	Round 2	3	4	4	4	5	5	4	3	4	4	5	5	4	5	4	3	4	6	76 -**149**
Chad Campbell	T78	Round 1	5	4	4	3	6	4	4	3	3	4	5	4	4	4	4	4	4	4	74
USA	**T91**	Round 2	4	5	4	4	5	4	4	4	4	5	3	5	3	4	4	3	5	4	75 -**149**
Achi Sato	T25	Round 1	4	4	3	3	3	4	4	4	5	5	5	5	3	4	5	3	4	4	71
Japan	**T91**	Round 2	4	4	4	4	6	4	4	4	4	6	4	5	4	5	4	4	4	4	78 -**149**
Loren Roberts	T78	Round 1	4	4	4	4	4	6	4	2	4	5	4	4	3	5	4	4	4	5	74
USA	**T91**	Round 2	4	3	5	4	5	5	4	3	5	6	4	5	2	3	5	4	4	4	75 -**149**
Steven Alker	T78	Round 1	5	3	4	4	4	4	5	3	4	5	4	4	3	5	4	3	5	5	74
New Zealand	**T91**	Round 2	3	5	4	4	5	4	4	4	4	3	4	5	3	6	6	3	4	4	75 -**149**
Adilson Da Silva	T78	Round 1	4	4	3	4	4	5	4	3	4	6	4	4	3	5	4	4	4	5	74
Brazil	**T91**	Round 2	4	6	4	4	5	5	4	2	4	4	4	5	3	4	4	3	4	6	75 -**149**
Stuart Appleby	T78	Round 1	3	4	5	4	4	5	4	3	4	6	4	5	3	5	4	3	3	5	74
Australia	**T91**	Round 2	4	5	4	4	5	5	4	3	4	4	4	5	3	6	4	3	3	5	75 -**149**
Geoff Ogilvy	T104	Round 1	3	4	5	4	5	6	3	3	4	7	3	5	3	5	4	3	4	4	75
Australia	**T91**	Round 2	4	4	5	4	5	4	4	3	3	5	4	4	4	6	3	4	4	4	74 -**149**
Hideto Tanihara	T39	Round 1	4	4	3	4	4	6	5	3	4	4	3	5	3	4	3	3	4	6	72
Japan	**T91**	Round 2	4	4	3	5	5	5	5	3	4	6	4	5	3	4	5	4	4	4	77 -**149**
Nick O'Hern	T25	Round 1	4	4	4	4	5	5	3	2	4	4	4	4	3	5	4	3	4	5	71
Australia	**T91**	Round 2	4	4	3	4	5	6	5	3	4	5	4	4	3	5	6	4	4	5	78 -**149**
Peter Baker	T60	Round 1	3	5	5	3	5	3	4	3	4	5	4	4	2	5	4	3	5	6	73
England	**T91**	Round 2	4	5	4	4	5	4	4	4	4	5	4	4	3	4	5	5	4	4	76 -**149**
Charl Schwartzel	T104	Round 1	4	4	5	4	4	5	4	3	4	4	4	5	3	5	5	3	4	5	75
South Africa	**T105**	Round 2	4	4	4	4	4	5	4	3	4	4	6	5	4	5	5	3	4	3	75 -**150**
John Daly	T78	Round 1	4	4	4	4	3	4	4	3	4	3	2	6	3	8	5	4	4	5	74
USA	**T105**	Round 2	5	4	4	4	4	6	4	3	5	4	5	6	3	5	4	3	3	4	76 -**150**

		HOLE	1	2	3	4	5	6	7	8	9	10	11	12	13	14	15	16	17	18	
PAR	POSITION		4	4	4	4	5	5	4	3	4	4	4	4	3	5	4	3	4	4	TOTAL
Bradley Dredge	T118	Round 1	4	4	4	4	5	5	4	3	5	5	5	4	3	5	4	4	4	4	76
Wales	**T105**	Round 2	3	5	4	4	5	4	4	4	4	5	4	4	3	4	4	4	5	4	74-150
Rory Sabbatini	T118	Round 1	5	4	5	4	5	4	3	3	5	5	5	4	3	4	4	3	5	5	76
South Africa	**T105**	Round 2	3	3	4	4	4	5	4	2	4	4	4	4	3	8	7	3	3	5	74-150
Graeme McDowell	T128	Round 1	4	5	4	3	4	7	5	3	4	4	4	5	3	5	5	4	4	4	77
Northern Ireland	**T105**	Round 2	4	5	4	3	6	4	4	4	4	5	4	4	3	4	4	3	4	4	73-150
Francesco Molinari	T118	Round 1	4	4	5	4	5	6	3	2	5	5	4	5	3	5	4	3	4	5	76
Italy	**T105**	Round 2	4	4	4	4	5	5	4	3	4	5	4	4	3	4	4	3	4	6	74-150
Paul Sheehan	T104	Round 1	4	4	4	4	4	4	3	4	5	4	5	4	4	5	5	4	4	4	75
Australia	**T105**	Round 2	5	4	5	5	5	4	4	3	4	5	4	4	3	4	4	4	4	4	75-150
David Higgins	T142	Round 1	4	4	5	4	4	5	4	6	4	5	4	4	3	5	4	4	5	5	79
Republic of Ireland	**T105**	Round 2	4	4	4	4	4	5	4	3	4	3	4	5	3	4	4	3	5	4	71-150
Matt Kuchar	T78	Round 1	4	4	5	3	4	6	3	3	5	5	4	4	3	5	4	3	4	5	74
USA	**T105**	Round 2	3	4	4	4	6	4	4	4	4	4	4	5	3	5	5	3	5	5	76-150
Richard Sterne	T118	Round 1	3	4	5	4	4	5	4	3	4	6	5	4	4	4	4	4	4	5	76
South Africa	**T105**	Round 2	4	4	4	4	5	5	4	3	3	4	4	5	3	4	4	4	5	5	74-150
Davis Love III	T142	Round 1	4	4	7	4	4	6	4	3	5	4	4	5	3	4	4	4	4	6	79
USA	**T105**	Round 2	3	4	5	3	5	5	4	2	4	5	4	4	2	4	5	3	4	5	71-150
Jeev Milkha Singh	T128	Round 1	3	4	5	4	5	5	4	3	4	5	5	4	3	5	4	3	6	5	77
India	**T105**	Round 2	4	4	3	5	5	4	4	3	4	6	3	5	4	4	4	3	4	4	73-150
Michael Putnam	T136	Round 1	4	4	5	4	4	5	3	5	5	5	3	5	3	6	5	3	5	4	78
USA	**T105**	Round 2	3	4	4	4	4	5	4	3	4	4	4	3	3	4	5	4	6	4	72-150
Spencer Levin	T118	Round 1	4	4	5	4	5	5	3	3	4	5	4	7	2	5	4	3	5	4	76
USA	**T105**	Round 2	4	5	3	5	4	6	4	3	5	4	4	4	2	4	4	4	5	4	74-150
Mattias Eliasson	T78	Round 1	3	4	5	4	5	5	4	3	4	5	4	4	3	5	4	4	4	4	74
Sweden	**T105**	Round 2	3	4	3	4	6	5	4	4	4	4	4	4	3	4	5	3	4	8	76-150
Richie Ramsay*	T118	Round 1	3	4	5	4	5	4	4	4	4	5	5	4	3	4	5	3	4	6	76
Scotland	**T120**	Round 2	4	4	4	4	4	5	4	4	4	5	5	5	3	4	4	3	5	4	75-151
Aaron Baddeley	T136	Round 1	3	4	4	4	4	5	4	5	8	4	4	4	3	5	4	3	4	6	78
Australia	**T120**	Round 2	4	3	4	4	4	6	4	3	4	4	4	5	3	5	4	3	4	5	73-151
John Bickerton	T104	Round 1	4	5	5	3	4	5	5	2	4	4	4	5	3	5	5	3	4	5	75
England	**T120**	Round 2	4	4	4	4	4	4	4	2	5	5	6	5	3	4	5	3	4	6	76-151
Stephen Ames	T150	Round 1	4	4	6	6	4	6	4	3	5	6	4	4	3	5	5	3	4	5	81
Canada	**T120**	Round 2	4	4	4	3	4	5	4	3	4	4	4	4	3	4	4	3	4	5	70-151
Robert Karlsson	T78	Round 1	4	4	4	4	4	4	4	3	4	5	5	4	3	5	5	4	4	4	74
Sweden	**T124**	Round 2	4	4	4	4	5	5	4	3	4	5	4	4	3	6	4	3	5	7	78-152
Robert Allenby	T60	Round 1	4	3	4	4	5	4	4	3	4	4	4	5	4	4	4	4	4	5	73
Australia	**T124**	Round 2	4	4	5	4	6	5	4	3	4	5	4	4	3	5	6	4	4	5	79-152
Yong-Eun Yang	T78	Round 1	4	4	4	4	5	4	5	3	4	3	4	5	3	5	5	4	3	5	74
South Korea	**T124**	Round 2	3	5	5	4	3	5	4	3	5	4	4	4	4	5	4	3	5	8	78-152
Kevin Harper	T128	Round 1	5	6	4	4	5	5	4	3	3	5	3	5	4	5	4	4	4	4	77
England	**T124**	Round 2	4	4	4	5	4	5	3	3	4	4	5	5	3	5	3	4	5	5	75-152
Oliver Wilson	149	Round 1	3	4	3	6	5	8	5	4	4	5	4	4	3	4	4	4	5	5	80
England	**T124**	Round 2	4	4	4	4	5	6	4	3	5	4	4	4	3	4	4	2	4	4	72-152
Nick Faldo	T142	Round 1	4	5	5	4	5	4	4	3	4	6	4	5	3	6	4	3	5	5	79
England	**T124**	Round 2	4	5	5	3	4	4	4	4	4	5	4	5	3	4	3	3	4	5	73-152

HOLE			1	2	3	4	5	6	7	8	9	10	11	12	13	14	15	16	17	18	
PAR	POSITION		4	4	4	4	4	5	4	3	4	4	4	4	3	5	4	3	4	4	TOTAL
Chih Bing Lam	T118	Round 1	5	5	4	4	5	5	4	4	4	6	4	4	3	5	3	3	4	4	76
Singapore	**T130**	Round 2	4	6	4	3	5	4	4	4	5	4	4	4	3	6	4	3	6	4	77-**153**
Seung-Ho Lee	T128	Round 1	4	5	4	5	4	5	5	3	4	5	3	6	3	4	4	3	4	6	77
South Korea	**T130**	Round 2	5	5	3	4	4	5	4	3	4	6	4	5	2	4	6	3	4	5	76-**153**
David Coupland*	T142	Round 1	3	6	6	4	5	4	3	3	5	5	3	5	3	5	6	3	5	5	79
England	**T130**	Round 2	4	4	3	5	4	4	4	3	5	4	5	5	2	5	4	3	5	5	74-**153**
Anthony Wall	T128	Round 1	4	4	4	4	5	5	3	5	4	4	4	5	3	5	4	4	4	6	77
England	**T130**	Round 2	4	4	4	4	4	5	4	3	4	5	4	5	3	5	5	3	4	6	76-**153**
Todd Hamilton	T150	Round 1	4	5	5	4	5	5	5	3	4	4	4	6	3	6	6	4	4	4	81
USA	**T130**	Round 2	4	4	4	4	3	4	4	2	5	4	4	5	4	6	3	2	5	5	72-**153**
David Shacklady	T118	Round 1	4	4	4	4	6	4	4	3	5	5	4	5	2	5	4	4	4	5	76
England	**T130**	Round 2	4	6	4	4	4	5	5	3	3	5	4	5	3	5	5	4	3	5	77-**153**
Dong-Hwan Lee	T104	Round 1	4	5	5	3	5	4	3	3	4	5	4	5	3	5	5	5	3	4	75
South Korea	**T130**	Round 2	3	4	4	4	6	6	4	3	5	5	5	4	4	5	4	3	4	5	78-**153**
Toshinori Muto	T78	Round 1	4	4	5	4	4	6	4	3	4	5	3	5	3	5	5	3	3	4	74
Japan	**T130**	Round 2	4	4	5	5	4	5	4	4	5	5	5	5	4	4	5	3	4	4	79-**153**
Mark Hensby	T142	Round 1	4	5	6	4	5	4	4	4	5	4	4	4	3	5	5	5	4	4	79
Australia	**T138**	Round 2	4	6	4	5	5	5	4	3	4	4	4	4	3	4	4	3	5	4	75-**154**
Paul Waring*	T78	Round 1	5	5	5	3	5	4	3	3	4	4	3	5	3	6	4	3	4	5	74
England	**T138**	Round 2	4	6	4	4	5	4	5	3	4	5	4	6	4	5	4	4	5	4	80-**154**
Steve Parry	T60	Round 1	4	4	4	4	5	6	4	3	5	5	3	4	2	5	4	3	4	4	73
England	**T138**	Round 2	3	7	5	5	5	5	4	4	5	4	6	4	3	4	4	3	4	6	81-**154**
Scott Laycock	T78	Round 1	5	4	4	4	5	6	4	3	4	6	4	4	3	4	3	3	4	4	74
Australia	**T138**	Round 2	4	5	4	4	5	5	4	3	4	6	3	5	4	5	5	3	6	5	80-**154**
Anders Hultman	T128	Round 1	4	5	4	4	4	5	4	4	4	5	5	4	2	5	4	3	4	7	77
Sweden	**T138**	Round 2	4	5	5	4	4	6	5	4	3	4	4	6	3	4	4	4	4	4	77-**154**
Jose-Filipe Lima	T104	Round 1	4	4	5	4	6	4	4	3	5	4	3	5	3	6	4	2	3	6	75
Portugal	**T138**	Round 2	4	5	5	4	4	6	4	3	4	4	4	4	4	5	5	3	4	7	79-**154**
Duffy Waldorf	T153	Round 1	4	4	4	4	5	5	5	4	4	6	4	6	3	5	5	3	5	6	82
USA	**144**	Round 2	4	4	5	4	3	4	3	5	5	4	4	6	2	4	5	2	4	5	73-**155**
Desvonde Botes	T136	Round 1	3	4	5	4	4	5	4	4	4	5	3	5	3	5	4	3	6	7	78
South Africa	**T145**	Round 2	4	5	4	5	4	6	3	4	3	5	3	6	4	5	5	3	5	4	78-**156**
Vaughn Taylor	T153	Round 1	4	4	7	3	4	4	5	3	4	6	5	5	3	5	3	5	5	6	82
USA	**T145**	Round 2	4	4	4	5	5	5	5	3	5	4	4	4	3	4	4	3	4	4	74-**156**
Justin Kehoe	T136	Round 1	4	4	4	4	4	5	4	3	5	6	5	5	3	5	5	4	4	4	78
Republic of Ireland	**T147**	Round 2	4	3	4	5	4	4	6	5	5	5	4	4	3	5	5	4	4	5	79-**157**
Douglas McGuigan	T128	Round 1	4	4	4	4	5	4	6	3	5	5	4	4	3	5	4	4	4	5	77
Scotland	**T147**	Round 2	5	5	4	3	6	5	5	2	5	6	5	5	3	5	5	4	3	4	80-**157**
Llewellyn Matthews*	T104	Round 1	4	5	5	4	6	4	4	3	5	4	4	5	2	5	4	3	4	4	75
Wales	**T149**	Round 2	4	4	5	4	5	4	4	5	5	4	5	5	4	5	6	3	5	6	83-**158**
Ben Bunny	T150	Round 1	4	5	4	4	5	5	3	4	4	7	4	5	3	5	5	4	5	5	81
Australia	**T149**	Round 2	5	5	4	4	5	4	4	3	4	5	4	5	3	5	4	3	5	5	77-**158**
Graeme Storm	T136	Round 1	4	4	4	3	5	5	4	3	5	5	4	4	3	5	5	3	4	7	78
England	**T149**	Round 2	3	4	4	5	4	7	4	2	4	7	4	4	4	5	5	3	5	6	80-**158**
Scott Drummond	T142	Round 1	4	4	5	3	4	8	4	3	4	5	4	4	4	5	5	3	5	5	79
Scotland	**T152**	Round 2	4	4	4	4	6	5	4	3	5	5	5	4	3	5	5	5	5	5	81-**160**

HOLE			1	2	3	4	5	6	7	8	9	10	11	12	13	14	15	16	17	18	
PAR	POSITION		4	4	4	4	4	5	4	3	4	4	4	4	3	5	4	3	4	4	TOTAL
Adam Groom	T142	Round 1	5	3	6	3	6	6	4	5	4	5	4	4	3	4	5	4	4	4	79
Australia	**T152**	Round 2	5	5	5	4	6	6	4	4	4	4	4	5	3	5	4	4	4	5	81 **-160**
David Gleeson	T155	Round 1	4	4	6	4	5	4	5	3	5	5	5	5	3	6	5	4	5	5	83
Australia	**T152**	Round 2	4	3	4	4	5	5	4	3	5	3	5	5	4	7	3	4		5	77 **-160**
Tony Jacklin	T136	Round 1	4	4	3	4	7	5	4	3	4	5	4	5	3	6	4	4	4	5	78
England	**155**	Round 2	4	5	5	4	5	6	5	4	4	4	4	5	3	7	4	3	5	5	83 **-161**
Ewan Porter	T155	Round 1	4	5	4	3	5	6	4	4	4	7	4	8	3	4	5	4	4	5	83
Australia	**156**	Round 2	6	4	5	4	4	4	4	3	5	5	5	5	3	6	5	4	4	3	79 **-162**

THE TOP TENS Courtesy of Unisys

Birdies
1. Andres Romero 18
1. Rich Beem 18
3. Jim Furyk 17
3. Chris DiMarco 17
3. Steve Stricker 17
6. Charley Hoffman 16
6. Hunter Mahan 16
6. Ian Poulter 16
6. Justin Rose 16
6. Retief Goosen 16
23. *Padraig Harrington* *13*

Pars
1. Adam Scott 54
2. Miguel Angel Jimenez 53
3. *Padraig Harrington* *52*
4. Zach Johnson 51
5. Markus Brier 50
5. Mark Calcavecchia 50
5. Paul Casey 50
5. Boo Weekley 50
9. Sergio Garcia 49
9. Ernie Els 49
9. Ben Curtis 49
9. Rod Pampling 49
9. Nick Watney 49

Bogeys
1. Jon Bevan 24
2. Fredrik Andersson Hed 23
3. David Howell 22
4. Anders Hansen 21
5. Alastair Forsyth 20
6. Luke Donald 19
6. Peter Hanson 19
8. Michael Campbell 18
8. Trevor Immelman 18
8. Mark O'Meara 18
8. Toru Taniguchi 18
8. Sandy Lyle 18
156. *Padraig Harrington* *4*

Double Bogeys/Worse
1. Kevin Stadler 6/1
2. Duffy Waldorf 5/0
2. Gregory Bourdy 2/3
4. Brian Davis 4/0
4. Seung-Ho Lee 4/0
4. Llewellyn Matthews 4/0
4. Adam Groom 4/0
4. Lucas Glover 4/0
4. Boo Weekley 4/0
4. Nick Dougherty 4/0
4. Raphael Jacquelin 3/1
4. Graeme Storm 2/2
20. *Padraig Harrington* *2/0*

Driving Distance
1. Sergio Garcia 307.9
2. Adam Scott 303.1
3. Pelle Edberg 302.8
4. Andres Romero 301.1
5. Lee Westwood 300.1
6. Fredrik Andersson Hed . 300.0
7. Stewart Cink 298.9
8. Boo Weekley 298.1
8. Angel Cabrera 298.1
10. Nick Watney 297.5
12. *Padraig Harrington* *296.9*

Fairways Hit
Maximum of 60
1. Brian Davis 46
1. Luke Donald 46
1. Lucas Glover 46
4. Hunter Mahan 45
5. Zach Johnson 44
5. Jim Furyk 44
5. Rich Beem 44
8. 7 players tied 43
37. *Padraig Harrington* *37*

Greens in Regulation
Maximum of 72
1. Lucas Glover 57
1. Hunter Mahan 57
3. Stewart Cink 52
4. Sergio Garcia 51
5. Pat Perez 50
5. John Senden 50
7. Miguel Angel Jimenez 49
7. Jerry Kelly 49
9. Richard Green 48
9. Trevor Immelman 48
9. K J Choi 48
12. *Padraig Harrington* *47*

Putts
1. Andres Romero 104
2. Pelle Edberg 108
2. Markus Brier 108
4. Retief Goosen 109
4. David Howell 109
6. Ernie Els 110
6. Chris DiMarco 110
8. *Padraig Harrington* *111*
8. Paul Broadhurst 111
8. Rich Beem 111
8. Thomas Bjorn 111
8. Raphael Jacquelin 111

Statistical Rankings
Courtesy of Unisys

	Driving Distance	Rank	Fairways Hit	Rank	Greens In Regulation	Rank	Putts	Rank
Fredrik Anderson Hed	300.0	6	34	47	37	62	116	26
Ross Bain	287.0	29	39	30	47	12	126	62
Rich Beem	285.1	34	44	5	41	47	111	8
Jon Bevan	250.9	70	40	22	34	66	117	33
Thomas Bjorn	277.1	47	36	41	30	70	111	8
Gregory Bourdy	263.5	69	34	47	39	54	113	17
Markus Brier	267.8	65	36	41	41	47	108	2
Paul Broadhurst	271.8	60	35	44	44	30	111	8
Jonathan Byrd	286.6	31	40	22	44	30	116	26
Angel Cabrera	298.1	8	33	56	45	21	120	46
Mark Calcavecchia	292.3	19	43	8	45	21	117	33
Michael Campbell	281.5	38	29	67	36	63	118	38
Paul Casey	296.3	14	40	22	47	12	122	57
K J Choi	279.5	43	41	17	48	9	116	26
Stewart Cink	298.9	7	29	67	52	3	120	46
Ben Curtis	270.3	62	43	8	47	12	115	19
Brian Davis	265.4	67	46	1	41	47	119	42
Chris DiMarco	286.9	30	38	33	40	52	110	6
Luke Donald	272.9	57	46	1	41	47	121	55
Nick Dougherty	295.4	16	34	47	44	30	117	33
Pelle Edberg	302.8	3	36	41	39	54	108	2
Ernie Els	290.9	22	31	64	44	30	110	6
Niclas Fasth	291.1	20	38	33	47	12	120	46
Alastair Forsyth	275.8	51	42	15	44	30	131	69
Mark Foster	276.1	50	27	70	41	47	115	19
Jim Furyk	285.1	34	44	5	45	21	117	33
Sergio Garcia	307.9	1	43	8	51	4	119	42
Lucas Glover	287.8	28	46	1	57	1	127	65
Retief Goosen	290.9	22	34	47	39	54	109	4
Richard Green	269.3	64	38	33	48	9	114	18
Anders Hansen	276.8	48	42	15	40	52	124	61
Peter Hanson	285.9	33	34	47	43	40	127	65
Padraig Harrington	296.9	12	37	37	47	12	111	8
J J Henry	297.1	11	43	8	45	21	119	42
Charley Hoffman	280.9	40	30	65	46	18	122	57
David Howell	264.3	68	34	47	33	69	109	4
Trevor Immelman	291.0	21	33	56	48	9	131	69
Raphael Jacquelin	279.4	44	40	22	34	66	111	8
Miguel Angel Jimenez	265.5	66	43	8	49	7	118	38
Zach Johnson	279.0	45	44	5	45	21	112	13
Jerry Kelly	275.1	53	37	37	49	7	126	62
Won Joon Lee	296.8	13	28	69	43	40	119	42
Tom Lehman	284.0	36	39	30	44	30	120	46
Sandy Lyle	284.0	36	33	56	34	66	118	38
Hunter Mahan	290.9	22	45	4	57	1	126	62
Paul McGinley	272.3	59	41	17	43	40	112	13
Rory McIlroy*	295.5	15	30	65	42	45	120	46
Shaun Micheel	273.0	56	43	8	45	21	123	60
Ryan Moore	288.4	27	34	47	39	54	115	19
Arron Oberholser	274.3	54	37	37	39	54	116	26
Sean O'Hair	274.1	55	40	22	39	54	127	65
Mark O'Meara	270.3	62	33	56	39	54	120	46
Rod Pampling	280.3	42	40	22	43	40	116	26
Pat Perez	290.3	25	43	8	50	5	120	46
Carl Pettersson	280.9	40	34	47	44	30	120	46
Ian Poulter	276.5	49	32	62	42	45	115	19
Andres Romero	301.1	4	32	62	44	30	104	1
Justin Rose	288.9	26	41	17	46	18	116	26
Adam Scott	303.1	2	33	56	39	54	112	13
John Senden	286.5	32	39	30	50	5	128	68
Vijay Singh	295.1	17	33	56	44	30	117	33
Kevin Stadler	281.4	39	41	17	43	40	120	46
Steve Stricker	278.8	46	40	22	46	18	115	19
Toru Taniguchi	272.8	58	40	22	35	64	115	19
Scott Verplank	270.4	61	38	33	35	64	116	26
Nick Watney	297.5	10	35	44	45	21	121	55
Boo Weekley	298.1	8	41	17	47	12	122	57
Mike Weir	275.3	52	34	47	44	30	112	13
Lee Westwood	300.1	5	37	37	45	21	118	38
Tiger Woods	294.8	18	35	44	45	21	115	19

Rank indicates position (including ties) after 72 holes.

NON QUALIFIERS AFTER 36 HOLES

Name	Driving Distance	Rank	Fairways Hit	Rank	Greens In Regulation	Rank	Putts	Rank
Steven Alker	277.5	126	25	2	16	136	58	31
Robert Allenby	281.3	109	17	98	20	60	63	130
Stephen Ames	287.5	83	22	18	20	60	61	87
Stuart Appleby	308.5	7	17	98	19	77	59	44
Aaron Baddeley	303.8	19	17	98	20	60	60	63
Peter Baker	291.8	60	19	63	17	122	58	31
Benn Barham	278.8	121	23	10	19	77	60	63
John Bickerton	247.3	155	14	140	19	77	60	63
Desvonde Botes	271.0	140	12	151	14	148	58	31
Ben Bunny	274.8	131	18	79	16	136	62	108
Chad Campbell	291.3	64	21	33	19	77	61	87
Darren Clarke	303.0	20	24	6	20	60	62	108
David Coupland*	269.8	142	18	79	19	77	60	63
Adilson Da Silva	252.0	154	20	43	19	77	62	108
John Daly	307.3	9	15	132	20	60	61	87
Bradley Dredge	292.0	58	17	98	17	122	58	31
Scott Drummond	288.8	76	18	79	13	152	61	87
Joe Durant	269.3	143	18	79	22	39	61	87
Johan Edfors	296.8	40	16	121	18	99	60	63
Mattias Eliasson	298.8	32	16	121	19	77	58	31
Nick Faldo	273.8	133	19	63	16	136	61	87
Ross Fisher	311.3	6	17	98	25	16	68	154
Peter Fowler	278.5	123	16	121	17	122	55	11
David Frost	268.3	145	18	79	20	60	62	108
David Gleeson	291.8	60	16	121	13	152	63	130
Adam Groom	294.8	46	10	153	11	156	61	87
Todd Hamilton	282.8	103	10	153	17	122	60	63
Kevin Harper	281.5	108	22	18	21	48	64	137
Gregory Havret	294.5	48	19	63	17	122	59	44
Mark Hensby	280.8	112	19	63	17	122	64	137
David Higgins	272.0	137	17	98	14	148	56	19
Charles Howell III	287.0	85	17	98	20	60	62	108
Anders Hultman	268.3	145	18	79	18	99	60	63
Toshi Izawa	280.5	114	19	63	19	77	62	108
Tony Jacklin	267.0	147	18	79	14	148	64	137
Robert Karlsson	305.0	16	14	140	19	77	64	137
Justin Kehoe	276.5	130	19	63	15	145	63	130
Tomohiro Kondo	296.8	40	21	33	19	77	59	44
Matt Kuchar	262.3	150	21	33	21	48	62	108
Chih Bing Lam	303.0	20	16	121	18	99	63	130
Paul Lawrie	321.5	1	18	79	23	27	65	144
Scott Laycock	266.5	148	15	132	15	145	58	31
Dong-Hwan Lee	285.8	94	21	33	16	136	61	87
Seung-Ho Lee	263.0	149	17	98	18	99	62	108
Justin Leonard	293.3	52	21	33	18	99	58	31
Spencer Levin	291.0	65	19	63	19	77	61	87
Jose-Filipe Lima	293.3	52	12	151	15	145	55	11
Davis Love III	305.5	13	24	6	22	39	65	144
Llewellyn Matthews*	288.8	76	17	98	18	99	62	108
Graeme McDowell	287.5	83	20	43	17	122	59	44
Douglas McGuigan	277.5	126	15	132	16	136	62	108
Phil Mickelson	307.3	9	18	79	23	27	65	144
Francesco Molinari	283.8	101	19	63	21	48	62	108
Colin Montgomerie	289.0	74	22	18	20	60	62	108
Toshinori Muto	289.3	71	17	98	19	77	64	137
Geoff Ogilvy	286.8	87	20	43	22	39	63	130
Nick O'Hern	289.3	71	19	63	22	39	65	144
Steve Parry	298.3	34	17	98	18	99	63	130
Tom Pernice Jnr	298.0	36	23	10	18	99	60	63
Terry Pilkadaris	281.8	107	19	63	19	77	60	63
Ewan Porter	279.0	119	8	156	12	154	61	87
Michael Putnam	289.5	69	14	140	18	99	61	87
Brett Quigley	280.8	112	20	43	24	19	64	137
Richie Ramsay*	282.0	106	17	98	17	122	59	44
Loren Roberts	258.0	152	20	43	18	99	59	44
John Rollins	288.5	78	16	121	18	99	60	83
Rory Sabbatini	294.0	51	21	33	17	122	57	21
Achi Sato	292.5	57	20	43	17	122	59	44
Charl Schwartzel	300.8	26	14	140	18	99	60	63
David Shacklady	279.3	118	14	140	18	99	64	137
Paul Sheehan	279.5	117	20	43	17	122	59	44
Jeev Milkha Singh	280.5	114	9	155	16	136	57	21
Henrik Stenson	289.8	67	17	98	20	60	60	63
Richard Sterne	293.3	52	14	140	18	99	60	63
Graeme Storm	255.3	153	13	148	12	154	53	4
Hideto Tanihara	242.0	156	17	98	21	48	62	108
Vaughn Taylor	272.5	136	21	33	18	99	62	108
David Toms	290.0	66	20	43	20	60	60	63
Duffy Waldorf	286.0	91	19	63	22	39	68	154
Anthony Wall	291.5	63	18	79	16	136	61	87
Paul Waring*	314.3	3	13	148	17	122	59	44
Drew Weaver*	299.5	29	18	79	16	136	58	31
Brett Wetterich	288.5	78	15	132	21	48	60	63
Oliver Wilson	274.0	132	18	79	18	99	61	87
Yong-Eun Yang	311.8	4	17	98	18	99	58	31
Matthew Zions	301.3	25	22	18	21	48	60	63

Rank indicates position (including ties) after 36 holes.

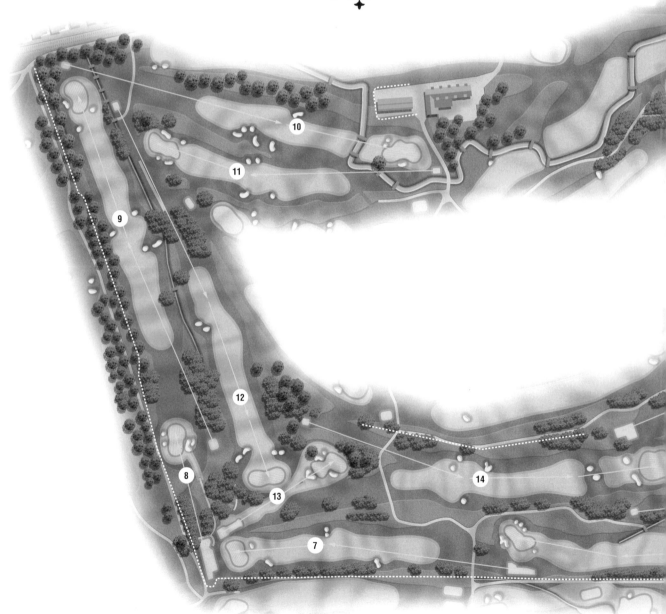

CARNOUSTIE
GOLF LINKS